A Day Without Mama

A True Story

BETH LENOR DUKES

A Day Without Mamma
by Beth Lenor Dukes

Editor: Loral Robben Pepoon, cowriterpro.com

Cover Art: Moriah Quint
Interior Art: Stephen Gregoire
Cover Design: Christine Dupre, vidagraphicdesign.com

ISBN-13: 978-0692168479 (Selah Press)
ISBN-10: 0692168478

Printed in the United States of America
Published by Selah Press

Dedication

To the little ones who experienced a childhood dictated solely by negligent adults,

and

To the many who loved me well and gave to me unselfishly,

and, of course,

To Thomas Alva Good who is my proof that what was meant for evil God has certainly turned into greatness.

Part 1

1

Between mountains lush with Rhododendron and towering, mighty oaks, is a land that has defeated scores of the heartiest of men. Robed in deceptive beauty, these majestic peaks of Eastern Kentucky are infamous. They have for centuries been known dually as a unique frontier and as a place of strangling poverty. Those hollows are filled with lost hope, deprivation, starvation, and lack. Many a hill is flecked with worn-down shacks whose cupboards are too often empty. Generations of ill-clad children and adults cling to the little they own having become accustomed to darkness and pain.

In spite of the strangling poverty—and likely because of the Cumberland Mountain's beauty and awe-inspiring landscape, every generation that desires to call it home begins with great determination to become the victor over destitution. Each man with or without a bride begins his story as it should begin. The frontier calls, and man answers.

The lives of dreamers and the pioneers are full of new beginnings, energized by love and adventurous determination. No one—not one soul—sets out to be taken captive or fall victim to the ACCUSER.

Her blue eyes were full of the hope and love common to most brides. His eyes were steady with the love and purpose of a groom eager to conquer the world on his bride's behalf. Together they could defeat any enemy. He had a plan, and with his bride at his side, they would take their place in time and history, ready for even the difficult times that come to all couples. Seated on horse-drawn cart, they journeyed beside crooked creeks along narrow mountain passages as old as the pictures drawn on the walls of the cave they took shelter in.

That new Cumberland Mountain sunrise would announce the couple's marital bliss, but those Eastern Kentucky peaks would hourly stand up to be reckoned with. Together he and she travelled on. In unison, they sang and planned and fell under the spell of happiness and purpose. Each day and night on this adventure to get to their future home, he whispered his devotion to her. She would confirm hers with joyful, tear-filled winks or a peck on the cheek.

The day came when a cabin was in sight and their wagon and horse could finally rest. It was a simple structure marked with the undeniable signs of abandonment. He was undaunted and promised to make the cabin sound and ready in short order. Her eager hands performed transforming miracles, thanks to the treasures brought forth from her wooden chest of hopes. It mattered not that neither bride nor groom brought one dollar of savings into the marriage. But each brought all they had.

The ACCUSER, the true king of Appalachian POVERTY, would receive no acknowledgement from this couple, for theirs was an especially strong and potent love. Their love could be food enough—it was shelter—steady and sure. This love was their hope in times of need. This love was the bank they planned to draw from—but …

Year by year, that dirt floor, one-room cabin dressed with calico curtains tied back at the windows witnessed the blessed gift of a new life. She blessed him with all of herself, which was more than she could afford. But did he keep vigil over the "blessings?" Her innocent heart knew all too well the innumerable broken promises he had laid at her feet. Each day she had to face these sorrows of disappointment alone.

Now to the Cauldron of Life, the Evil Accuser is adding another hideous ingredient to POVERTY, but it will not be the last. Stirred in are BROKEN

PROMISES to her innocent heart, followed by the SORROWS OF DISAPPOINTMENT.

Yet in the faces of those children was the reflection of the honor and dignity that she had infused into her union with their father. Ralph and Ross, two boys had come first, then came loving, steady Margaret. Three more life-loving boys followed: Thomas, Brooks, and baby Toy. She nurtured and sang and mothered and sang … and prayed with desperate tears on her cheeks.

But it was her life that was being spent. Lavishly spent. Mama got sick—so sick. Ralph and Ross helped Margaret with chores and with the babies. Thomas attended to his mother. He did his best to comfort her, paying no attention to the reality of how often she was overcome with pain—the inconsolable kind of pain.

The constant state of lack was noticed at the table and accepted in the faint glow of the oil lamp that illuminated the corner where she sat to mend their threadbare clothing. No father told the children stories. No husband shared her burden. No partner comforted her or tenderly stroked her worried brow. Her love had indeed been traded for a jug.

The children's father went missing just when Mama's cries got the loudest. Thomas was often found sitting by her bed singing to her. More often than not, his tears washed his little face as he watched her face in the lamplight. It got so dark when the oil ran out, and his older siblings were taking care of chores and babies. He was the one left with no one to tuck him into bed. There was no one to reassure him that the dark wasn't going to last forever.

The Cauldron of Life was DARK, too. Not the same kind of DARK in which those mountains were shrouded or the kind of dark that exists at midnight, but A DARK PRESENCE OF HEAVY MISERY. Thomas was powerless to stop the sun from going down, and he was powerless to stop the sinister stirring of the black brew.

Thomas wasn't told by anyone that his Mama was dying—but he could smell it. On that dreaded day, people—strangers—filled the house, and wagons filled the yard. Under every tree, a group of men were smoking or chewing and debating in low, hushed tones. And then the Preacher Man appeared as if from thin air.

Thomas remembered Mama taking him to a neighbor's house once to have "home church." Mama had gathered all her children to go to this event. She carried baby Toy in the sling that she often used working in the garden or washing at the creek. Margaret skipped along holding Brooks's little hand and the older boys—Ross, Ralph, and Thomas—lumbered along. Sometimes a piggyback ride was given to Brooks. Ralph and Ross helped carry Toy. The troup had to stop often along this journey. Mama was sick already, but "praying," she said, "makes me stronger."

But there would be no more "home church". There would be no more praying—and Mama was not strong. She was gray-colored. And she was SILENT! Her Bible lay next to her open still to the last pages Thomas had struggled to read to her. His ears were ringing with the confusion of voices as he strained to hear again her last words to him. "Thomas, I love you, but Jesus loves you more that I ever could."

"No, Mama, I love you more."

Had she said good night or goodbye?

DEATH was stirring the Cauldron, and to it, was added ABANDONMENT.

Thomas could smell it now. It was so pungent that he nearly vomited, but there was no time. DEATH waits for no one, and Mama's lifeless body went into the pine box and was lowered right into that thieving black hole in the cold ground. Margaret was sobbing. Ralph and Ross just hung their heads in painful silence.

Brooks stood still as long as he could with a stick in his hand, looking at the adults standing at the edges of that hole. Then there came a point when this little boy could stand the silence no longer. His little heart spoke up in a tender yet demanding voice: "Stop it, stop it, that's MY MAMA!" he said as he ran slapping that stick against the legs responsible for being so cruel. He was too little to understand that no one had power over that black hole.

The sun was gone. The day had gone, and as usual, there was no father to light the lamp. On this broken, dark night, there was no voice to speak to the hideous blackness that had come upon them all. Some things never change. Oh, how alone Thomas felt, and as he sat in the cabin where his Mama's life was hopelessly absent, he buried his tear-soaked face into her quilt desperately breathing in and out. The smell of her was in the fibers, and for a blink in time, her warmth was there too. His body shook with the sorrow and the loss forced on him. Would there ever be a night that wasn't so dark?

Mourning did not prevent the new morning. It was still dark outside when Thomas heard his name. His ears could discern that familiar harsh and cutting voice. Father beckoned, and many a beating had taught Thomas never to be slow. He felt vulnerable and unprotected even though he stood in that familiar one-room cabin. Thomas's eyes scanned the table, then Mama's rocking chair, and the short stools that the children took turns using when they ate a meal. His gaze quickly landed on the usual sleeping place of his siblings—three beds that lay end to end, lined up along the back wall. Now real FEAR was setting in. The bed Margaret and Brooks shared with Toy was utterly stripped bare. *Where was Margaret? Where was Brooks and Toy?* Even Ralph and Ross stood there dumbfounded, looking at each other for answers.

Ralph, Ross, and Thomas then united at the end of the table, just in time to seize one another's hand. Their father had entered the cabin. His speech was directed at all three of them—only what he was saying was ridiculous! They were going to be leaving. By themselves. They were "grown-up now," he said.

Thomas was nowhere near grown up—he was only seven years old! He could barely milk a cow or help carry the water up the hill. And he most definitely could not plow. He was too little. He was never allowed to go down the mountain by himself—Mama said he was too young!

But this was a day without Mama.

Just now outside the cabin was a stranger's voice. Their father had left Ross, Ralph, and Thomas standing in their dark cabin with instructions to "wait right chere' till I send for ye." Ralph looked around for something to eat, and quickly handed a chunk of cornbread to his brothers. "Quick! Stuff half of it in yur mouth and the other in yur pocket. I have a sick feelin' this is the last meal for a long time." Ralph was always insightful but never selfish.

Thomas was absorbing the worried look on Ross's face and simultaneously worrying about what his father was doing outside with the stranger. The cabin door opened and with its opening came an air of revelation. His father's chilling, sharp voice jolted his mind back from the shadows. "Thomas, you git up in Clifton's wagon now. He's gonna give you a room. You'd best herry and mind what he says." And that was the last time Thomas got any instructions from his father. He was finished with Thomas in every way.

The Cauldron's brew of DEATH and POVERTY now included the cruelest dose of REJECTION.

Almost to spite the deep heartache felt by Thomas, the sun began to rise.

2

The wagon wheels began to turn, and Thomas kept his eyes fixed on the cabin door. However violent and desperate the cabin was most of the time, it had still been his only home. His mind was flashing with the memories of his siblings and Mama. The separation from them began to create a great pain in his heart, yet he mustered all his strength to keep his focus on that cabin door. He was determined to imprint its memory on his heart more than anything else. The wagon kept bumping along that dirt mountain ridge road with Thomas watching until home was completely out of sight.

Thomas's heart ached and his eyes strained for one last glimpse of his brothers. He had been the first to leave, and bad things usually happened to the boys when their father was at home. Thomas's head went dizzy with the possibilities. He prayed that Ralph and Ross would remember not to make their father angry. To be separated from them at any time was uncomfortable, but knowing the consequences of life-long interactions with an angry and often drunken man tore at Thomas's heart with real physical pain.

Who was this Clifton? He had never laid eyes on him before, but the past day's events overshadowed everything. It was just yesterday that the family had marked Mama's death by gathering under a tree. The shadow of strangers and the shadow of the black hole with that box going down, down, down meant she wasn't coming back—she couldn't come back. That event overshadowed everything. It was Thomas's broken heart that insisted on remembering no more—for now. It would be best to close his eyes and stop crying.

Thomas did not recall this man's presence ever being at the cabin, and his face was not easily forgotten. But then everything was happening so fast. He wasn't sure what was real and what was pain.

SUFFERING was vigorously stirring the Cauldron this time and Thomas's stomach could not manage the smell of life.

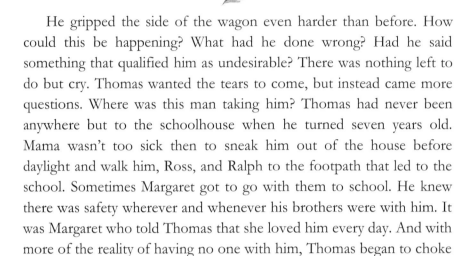

He gripped the side of the wagon even harder than before. How could this be happening? What had he done wrong? Had he said something that qualified him as undesirable? There was nothing left to do but cry. Thomas wanted the tears to come, but instead came more questions. Where was this man taking him? Thomas had never been anywhere but to the schoolhouse when he turned seven years old. Mama wasn't too sick then to sneak him out of the house before daylight and walk him, Ross, and Ralph to the footpath that led to the school. Sometimes Margaret got to go with them to school. He knew there was safety wherever and whenever his brothers were with him. It was Margaret who told Thomas that she loved him every day. And with more of the reality of having no one with him, Thomas began to choke with the pain of rejection.

Where was Mama now? Could she see him with the tears on his face? Thomas was confident that he would never see her again, and yet, she had said many times that they all would be together in Heaven very soon. But where was Heaven? And how could it be "soon?" Brooks and Baby Toy and Margaret and Ross and Ralph were not with him, and they were not together. He was going toward Dark Ridge with a man whose face did not give the appearance of someone who wanted to go to Heaven right this minute.

Clifton never spoke a word, nor did he ask Thomas any questions. Thomas was too young and too innocent to have guessed the purpose of this journey. His mind was strictly focused on remembering. He could remember Mama's face light up when he "helped" by chasing baby Toy while she cooked. He remembered her strong words, "Thomas, as long as you live, never lie, 'speshly to yourself." What an odd thing to say, and it was even more strange that he recalled it now—when he was headed to a place that he had never seen—a place where he did not want to go. It was no lie that Thomas didn't want to be in that wagon.

Thomas had wearily and sorrowfully climbed into that strange wagon just as the sun was coming over the ridge. This journey was to begin regardless of any preferences Thomas had. Life had changed because of grief and loss—weights that Thomas felt to his bones. The wagon moved steadily forward on this unknown road. It was natural for him to fall in and out of sleep in the silence, and in his sorrow, he fell in and out of the grieving when logic reminded him that all the days to come were going to be a day without Mama.

As the sun continued its journey into night time, the night brought a darkness of its own. The darkness that had gathered around the trees had gathered around his soul. It was the kind of night that closes around a person seeking to forever erase the possibility of comfort or the light of hope. Tragically, Thomas had long since closed his eyes to this monster of necessity and of certain doom. His condition was grief-stricken and physically sick, and this seven-year-old boy curled into a little ball, hoping the nightmare would soon end.

The wagon afforded not one ounce of comfort for Thomas. There was no blanket, nor was there even a pillow of hay on which to rest his little frame. He had left the only home he had ever known with the only clothes he owned—the ones on his back. And no shoes. Tears washed his face as reality soaked into his soul. He had no brother or sister to comfort him along this journey. He was alone, abandoned, and probably forgotten about already—by all accounts.

Just when the wheels of his mind could go no faster, the wagon wheels stopped. His heart wished to be taken back to the cabin—no matter what might have been his plight. But he was not in charge. In the dark reality, he bolted upright—startled and watchful.

He looked around in this new dark noticing a shadowy figure. It was definitely a woman. She carried a lit lantern and a sense of duty. *Maybe she will speak to me,* Thomas hoped. He waited for someone to tell him what was going to happen to him next, but the silence continued.

In the lamplight, he could just make out a few features of this woman. And he was frightened. Clifton turned around on the wagon bench as he spoke, "You two head ta bed. Daylight'll come sooner than we want it to. Viney, you git the boy to his room like we planned." That was all. He said not a syllable more. No word escaped her lips, so Thomas let himself out of the wagon bed, and with aching legs and head, he followed the woman's backside.

They walked along a path on into the woods a bit. Thomas had to concentrate on her back so that he wouldn't get left behind. It was as if she forgot that he was even there. The lantern glowed and swung back and forth, but not in such a way as to give Thomas a hint of where he was going. This woman, "Viney," wasn't letting any cat out of any bag. He knew he could count on that!

More walking, no talking, more darkness, no illumination. Strangers and strangeness. Weary and heavyhearted, Thomas struggled to stay alert. Putting one foot in front of the other was barely manageable. And then, the lantern ceased its swinging, and Viney stepped aside. As she reached into her apron pocket, he could finally make out the outline behind her shoulders. The wooden door was unlocked with a key the woman held. It seemed as quickly as the key turned in the lock, she thrusted it back into her skirt pocket with hateful passion. "This is yer room. Come daylight I'll fetch ye for breakfast." She waited for him to step inside the black space.

Thomas's footstep made an empty sound. And then the door was shut behind him. And of course, it locked. There was nothing left for Thomas to do but drop to the floor. He crawled forward hoping to find a bed or at least straw ticking to lie on. With frantic groping, he searched with his little hands in the darkness too bewildered to notice that it was not an earthen floor but wood-planked.

Without missing its opportunity to menace, the Cauldron stirred, sending a reminder of Thomas's real status in life—REJECTED.

He crumpled onto the bed of ticking and sobbed for who knows how long.

3

A familiar sound pried the boy's eyes open. A rooster's crow. Thomas lie flat on his back looking up at a low ceiling of gray-brown boards. Where was the light coming from? A small square high up on the wall behind him confirmed that he was not at home in the cabin. Nothing in this small room was right. It could never be like home. He rolled over, desperately wanting sleep to make everything go away, but the key in the lock reminded him of what had happened before. "Boy, food. Come quick, now. He don't take kindly ta havin' ta wait for meals."

Thomas stepped through the now-opened door and was shown the outhouse. Viney waited for him to finish, and the two of them marched to the well for washing. She had already poured a basin full for herself, and it was made clear that from this point on, he had to take care of himself. There was a fresh sense of alertness in Thomas. It did not come from the cold splash of water on his young face. No, it was something in the air—an attitude of the property on which he stood.

A new ingredient was being stirred in to the Cauldron. What was before him resembled a common component in a nightmare—DESPAIR. Its appearance is often disguised, but not this time.

Nothing lovely, nothing lively emitted from the house in front of him. Larger than life loomed this "house," for no one would dare call it a "home." It was being choked to death by vines. They pierced through the very fibers of the gray clapboards. Never a drop of paint nor any embellishment had come near. No—no hope of that. Every board was deeply grooved and dry-looking—like Viney's face.

Hopeless looking gables poked out of the sharp roofline. All of the windows looked asleep, not just because of the layers of dirt, but because they sagged oddly. All manner of life had likely paraded in front of this "house" without it welcoming anyone or anything. A porch went from what looked like could have been a front door, reaching around one corner.

With another sobering look, Thomas spied two big chains around two of the porch posts. Thomas wondered, *Whar are the dawgs 'at go ta them chains?*

Thomas was just about to ask his question when Viney groveled, "Boy, come 'his away. Clifton'll be awantin' his food so we'd best git our eat'n over with. We've got chores ahead a us."

Being served breakfast may have seemed like a genuine act of love if the food had been tasty or if the dish on which he ate was clean. But instead of feeling loved, Thomas felt as if he had been slapped or something. *When Mama had food fer us, hit was always good and we had fun cleanin' 'em dishes.* A tear and a lump in his throat reminded him of this day without Mama. Thomas ached to see his siblings' faces at breakfast, but instead everything he looked at was layered in dirt. His food looked as dirty as Viney's petticoat that dragged along the floor. The food tasted as bad as it looked.

Viney ate the way most mountain women eat—standing up. When she had finished, she threw the dishes in the washbasin and headed out the back door. Thomas knew what time it was when he spied that sunbonnet on her back. "Time ta be done eatin', boy." She had already pulled up the bonnet and put a plug of tobacco in her mouth. There was obviously not going to be any fun today.

Chores. He had his own at home. But what did Clifton and Viney expect of him? *Mama said she liked the way I stacked wood. That's sumthin' I did fer her and she always let me he'p on washday. But what day is this?* Thomas was wandering around in his thoughts when a real slap came to the back of his head. It was Clifton!

"Boy, 'round here, ye git t' eat 'cause ye done yer work. Now, I bin gen'rus wid ye so fur but ye best git things straight, right chere and now!" His rough voice was getting louder and louder, and his finger kept poking Thomas's chest, "I ain't yer friend. I gave ye a room, but hit t'weren't free."

The *truth* was finally out of the bag. Thomas was young and innocent in most things, but he was not stupid. Experience is a teacher. But so is FEAR, and when you put those two teachers together, their lessons are most often painful. Thomas had years of experience keeping out of trouble when FEAR was the teacher. Now that Clifton had shown his true identity in that short exchange, Thomas was more than convinced that it would be up to him and him alone to stay alive. He was determined to stay alive!

Clifton was a tall man with big ears and bigger hands. Thomas was also determined to stay clear of those giant hands. His own father had smaller hands, but they were still effective. The difference in the sizes of those two men didn't matter when Thomas considered their actions. He realized instead that they had the same anger, the same attitude, and the same results! There was not going to be any love at this house. Not even if there was a woman around. Clifton and Viney were the same to him.

4

One of the characteristics of Dark Ridge was its many hills. To have a crop of any size, a farmer in these hills had to be willing to clear out a lot of trees or have more than one field to harvest. The latter was the most common solution. Clifton's cornfield was sewn in such a way as to wrap around a small ridge and crowd right up to the tree line—snake-like.

Row upon row of corn stalks met Thomas daily. He had never seen so much corn in one place before in his life. He was pulling corn and tossing it into piles to be thrown onto the wagon beds. He pulled the lower ears while tall Viney took them off the upper part of the stalks. They worked together for weeks without any natural conversation. Clifton had made both his and Thomas's purpose clear, and conversation was not of any use. Clifton didn't ever speak more than two sentences together—not even to Viney. It was Clifton's job to gather the piles of corn ears into the wagon and haul them off. End of story.

But where this harvest was being taken and stored was a mystery to Thomas. The wagon was always empty at the end of the day. Most certainly, the wagon made multiple daily trips to the field during harvest time. They all rode in silence back to the house. No information slipped from either Clifton's or Viney's lips. Each night as he washed himself behind the outhouse, Thomas pondered: *The barn is only big enough fer the mules, wagon, and cow. How could thar be any room fer all that corn? ... I know! "Clifton sells it to the neighbors ... nope, no neighbors. Maybe he takes it ta town? But that would take all day ... not 'nough time.*

The lack of food and pangs of hunger in Thomas's stomach could be quieted for a time by the distraction of the missing harvest. All Thomas got for dinner was a cold chunk of meat and one cold ear of corn—even after all that hard work. To have a warm glass of milk and dry, old biscuits was a treat. Most days Thomas and Viney didn't even stop for the noonday meal, but they simply ate whatever Viney had in her basket. Then it was off to that little room to be locked away until the rooster crowed—again.

TIME. By ancient definition, one sunset to the next. Mountain folks start marking the time at sunrise, and then work until the sun is just setting, so that you wake the next day to do the same thing. And it repeats and repeats. So for Thomas, all the days ran together. But Thomas's needs were much different from Clifton and Viney. He needed TIME to be on his side.

Nothing else was going his way, and it made sense to him to look to TIME for answers. Surely TIME would fix the cuts on his hands and legs from the cornhusks. TIME would likely cure the ache in his body when he lay down at night. So, would TIME take on the responsibility of making his broken heart new again? Was it possible that TIME was the source for love and kindness? Would TIME be the one to give Thomas permission to see Brooks or Toy or Margaret or Ross? What about Ralph? Only TIME could answer for itself. Honestly, he felt like his life was answering to something or someone else besides TIME.

Somehow Thomas managed to be pleasant when doing his chores. He often hummed a familiar tune that he had heard around the home cabin or he sang one of the school songs. Ross used to sing with him when they used the two-man saw. *Boy, how I could make chore time fly with them tunes.* Against those hills, echoes of voice and bird song were inspiring. The sweet song of the wood hen was one of the only friendly sounds he encountered. The only human voice was that of his own and the occasional bark or growl from the two adults always watching him. He recalled Mama's words: "Music is everywhar ... There is always a song ta be heard. Always a song ta be sung." *Yep! That's what she says ... She did say that.* And only Heaven knows the hurt that remembrance brought.

It was a blessed thing that Thomas had helped his Mama on

washday. He had to do all his own washing now—not that there was much to wash. On the day that he stole TIME to wash, he stayed hidden under the tattered quilt from his straw bed. Never did Viney make Thomas wash his clothes. It wasn't her way. Oh, she was diligent in the execution of her duties to Clifton. She kept Thomas working in the field until all of the corn was harvested. She never gave Thomas a hint of what was to be expected of him the next day.

Viney was faithful … to the secrets—Thomas could feel them. He had grown to find comfort in her distance. Somehow it felt safer to leave her be. It scared him to think too long on what those eyes were really trying to communicate. An awful lot was said in what she did. Or didn't do. Nothing she wore even remotely gave him the impression of freshness, nor did she show a healthy respect for what she had. There was truly no respect for life or for Thomas. Instead, there was a sickening absence of a love of life.

5

All of life's ingredients continued to simmer in the Black Cauldron. What occupied Thomas's days was strictly labeled SURVIVAL. SELFISHNESS was now to keep vigil over this personal brew—relentless vigil.

Thomas undressed each night in the room Clifton "gave" him. His pants and shirt were carefully placed near the door. Everything had to be ready. Ready for anything. But on this night, his body and limbs twitched with fatigue, and his stomach loudly reminded him of the absence of food. When his body and limbs didn't move as much, his mind climbed and searched for treasure in his thoughts. *I noticed 'em squirrels sure was busy today. Workin' on they's own harvest. Jumpin' from tree ta tree. Chatterin' 'bout their piles a nuts. Ain't they a cleaver bunch? Wonder what kind of a winter we'll have? Mama told us they was a good example of how God takes keer of us all.* His pants were holey and too short now. It was a miracle that his shirt was still intact. What worried him most was longjohns—or lack thereof. Winter came quickly after harvest, sometimes.

Visions of the old rocking chair where Mama would work on the mending of his family's clothes by lamplight moved forward in his mind. With his worries heavy on him, Thomas squeezed his eyes shut. There Mama sat with her work in her small hands. He was once again back in his home cabin where he had seen her many a late night in that rocker. Humming and tapping her foot. Her face alone was a unique gift of comfort. So was her sweet voice as it sang,

"I'm just a poor wayfaring stranger
While traveling through this world alone
There is no sickness, toil or danger
In that bright land to which I go

I'm goin there to see my mother
I'm goin' there no more to roam
I'm only going over Jordan
I'm only going over home

I know dark clouds will gather o'r me
I know my way is rough and steep
But golden fields lie out before me
And weary eyes no more shall weep"

"Don't cry, Mama," Thomas said.

"But they's happy tears, love. I'm all right."

"I'm tired and hungry, Mama."

"It'll be over soon, son. Let me stitch up one
more leettle hole, hon'. Close yer eyes. Settle
down in the keevers, listen close, now."

And then her sweet voice was singing again. With severe hunger
bearing down on Thomas, he was frantically hoping to be consoled by
his mother. But he would forever be without her.

"I want to wear that crown of glory
When I get home to that bright land
I want to shout Salvation's story
In concert with that blood-washed band

I'm going there to see my Savior
Who shed for me His precious blood
I'm only goin' over Jordan

I'm only goin' over home

I'll soon be free from earthly trials
This form will rest beneath the sod
I'll drop this cross of self-denial
And enter in my home with God

I'm going there to see my Savior
To sing His praise forevermore
I'm only going over Jordan
I'm only going over home"[1]

"Good-bye, dear Thomas."

"Mama ... Mama ... MAMA ..."

6

Thomas's chores after corn harvest consisted of hoeing up the potatoes, making piles, and then bagging them into burlap sacks. His strength would often fade with the lack of food, BUT if he had to sit down, his eyes were always at attention! Thomas could never be sure just when Clifton would quickly appear ... spirit-like.

Viney took harvest work seriously. But one day, her actions confused Thomas. She gave him a very poor excuse of a knife. "Ye must never leave hit in the field. They ain't free an' we cain't have thangs ta go ta rottin' in the field." And off she went leaving him with those long rows of vegetables. After the sweet potato row came the butternut and acorn squash row.

With this small knife, he would cut the vegetables off their vines and stack them side-by-side in a nest of hay. Even the gourds were ready. One of the gourds had wrinkles, like Clifton's forehead when he got angry. Several gourds he found had cloth strips tied in places so as to reshape them for cups or ladles or bowls.

On rainy days, Thomas was locked in his room with a bushel basket of the beans to string. *Mama called these "leather britches." We all worked on our own string. Mama would clap and smile when she hung all the "leather britches" on thur hooks in the attic. One time we dried apples. What was 'at woman's name ... brought us apples 'at time? Reba, no ... Rachel ... no but boy they was great. By Jimminy, I wish I had one apple just now. A Winesap apple—that's hits name. Came from North Car'lina. Over the high mountains. Mama turned some of 'em into pies.* He smelled the air. His mouth was really watering by then. *But what good is wishin' or hopin' in this place?* It only brought on more disappointment. Next would come the frustration, not to mention the dependable reminder of an empty stomach. He had come to realize that some things might never change.

Some changes did occur. Fall came, and with it came the crisp air and coloring of the leaves. God painted even the hills of Dark Ridge. Clifton and Viney could not control that. To Thomas, it seemed more lonely than ever. For days, he was the only human on the property during the daylight. Food was left in Viney's basket on the front porch. Clifton would have already milked the cow, hitched the team to the wagon, and headed to points unknown. After washing his face and eating a dry breakfast, he was marched back to his room.

One morning when Thomas was pulling on his britches, he heard Clifton and Viney talking near his door. "Fetch the wheelbarra'. I gotta get this venison to the smokehouse."

A deer—MEAT!

Thomas's head buzzed with the news and his feet did a jig. *Yippee! I cain't believe hit!* He pressed his ear to the door and could finally hear the key in the lock. As the door opened wide, he jumped back. Shocked. What greeted him was not pleasant. Clifton was spattered and smeared with blood, and the deer carcass was swinging and violently jerking with each sawing motion. Headless, it was hanging from two big chains in the oak tree.

Thomas could hear its bones snapping from the vigorous blows and a ripping sound was piercing his conscience. Too much before breakfast. Thomas's knees buckled as he silently worried, *How can I eat, now? And if'n I don't—I'll have ta work without food. If I can't keep up, he'll beat me, again.* Off he ran to the outhouse, hoping the cold air and solitude would be the right combination for his queasy stomach.

Viney had her hands full helping Clifton at the smokehouse. As their backs stayed turned, Thomas slipped out and washed himself at the well. The cold water was a real blessing this time. He kept a watchful eye as Clifton took the deer hide, stretched it, and nailed it on the barn wall to dry. As they moved toward the house, Thomas ducked behind the outhouse, staying clear of Clifton's dangerous, bloody hands and Viney's cruel secrets.

The two adults marched towards the house. Viney went inside while Clifton remained out-of-doors and removed the washtub from its hanging spot on the house wall. Thomas could see plenty from his hidden position behind the outhouse. Clifton's next move was to remove his overalls and wait for Viney. There he stood in his underclothes. Out she came with a large steamy pail of water. Clifton stepped into the washtub and stilled himself. Viney perched herself on the old stump, ready to pour water over him to wash his nearly naked body.

There was something in this scene that held Thomas's attention. Had he seen this before? Of course not. As that water poured out and down Clifton's head, it mixed with the blood, making crimson rivulets down his brow and cheeks. The liquid stained Clifton's underwear.

A twisted and evil look was coming from Clifton's features. His hair was matted and stood up with thorn-like spikes that poked out of his forehead and crown. And under his breath, Thomas revealed what image had popped into his mind, "The thief, on the cross." It was the only picture in Mama's Bible that he could not stand to look at. He knew the story well. That man who would not say he was sorry, because he was a man without any love for anyone. He was a man who was guilty beside Jesus who was not—a man just like Clifton who was no different from his own father! All three of them were guilty of everything!

He flung himself to the ground, and grabbing his stomach groaning, he thought, *Jest like 'at picture, hit's jest like 'at picture* … And then came the awful retching.

Physically, Thomas could do nothing to change the scene before him. It was sickeningly obvious—hopelessly obvious—that the most important changes would never come. How much more was he going to have to endure? He began to shake violently as his young mind sought a ray of hope—but could find none. He could see nothing, nor could he find anything familiar. He felt like he was a stranger to himself.

He used to feel so happy when his days were filled with the love of Mama and her easy, gentle, clean presence. Her absence was the absolute truth that brought such deep sobs that, despite all his efforts, his little body began to shake even harder.

Just like any seven-year-old, Thomas wanted his Mama to comfort him. He desperately wanted to call her name, as he had done so many nights in the beginning. This time, it was too much heartache to face. She was not coming. She couldn't. No one was coming. No one cared. No one even remembered his existence. This was the truth. Better face it, right here and now before he made any more foolish assumptions. *Whar 'ere ya? Is anybody thar?* His thoughts questioned. An answer was coming. It came in the form of a song, a song that swept over him, like a merciful warm blanket. He was on his face, crouched into the dirt, alone. From the shadows of his memory, the song kept coming. The song he had learned to sing to his Mama when she was vomiting with her pain.

> "Through many dangers, toils, and snares
> I have already come;
> 'tis grace hath brought me safe thus far,
> and grace will lead me home."[2]

Whar 'ere you? Is anybody thar? I cain't see yer face. Hit's so dark ... His lonely, desperate thoughts and his sobbing eventually softened to gentle, surrendered crying.

And the Cauldron simmered on while LONLINESS and SORROW stoked the fire.

7

On a day before the rooster crowed, in the dark hours before dawn, she came for him. Dressed with her woolen shawl crossed over her chest, and fastened to her waist was "The Belt." But this had new meaning—if she had "The Belt," that meant Clifton was not going to be around. Viney waited with the lantern for Thomas to finish his usual morning routine. Finally she spoke, "Boy, we're headin' out." She laid sacks across his shoulders and across his body strung the water jug. The biting cold nipped at his shins and knees.

Viney whisked into the kitchen and came out with the rifle on her back and the bullet pouch tied to "The Belt." The night had ushered in a change on the land for a deep frost was crunching under their feet.

Thomas followed as usual, not knowing where he was going or what they were about to do. He had become conditioned to not being permitted to know anything. That mystery had begun the day Thomas had been put in their wagon—that first day without Mama.

The Cauldron simmered on with another layer of SECRETS.

Thomas had taken it upon himself to snag scraps of deer hide to fashion some sort of foot protection. As he gathered pieces of the deer hide, he thought of when he had worn moccasins for the first time. *Mama once made moccasins for Ross. I got ta wear 'em when he growed out of 'em. An 'at was so long ago.* With that memory's inspiration he worked, in secret, using his small knife. He cut long laces, put holes in the skins, and placed his foot on top. Guided by the holes, Thomas laced them up his foot and then behind the ankle securing the moccasin with a firm knot on the side of the ankle. *Beats cold toes, it does!* Clifton and

Viney either never noticed or they checked off the responsibility, seeing that the seven-year-old picked up the slack.

Viney carried a tied bundle in her left hand and her food basket over her right arm. She was able to keep her hands warm under the shawl, but Thomas struggled. He struggled to keep warm, he struggled to keep pace, and he struggled with FEAR. He struggled in silence, for he had become an expert in silence having been taught "to keep yer mouth shet lessin' ye want yer head knocked clean off"—so he did "keep it shet." Therefore, his struggle continued, internally. Her silence naturally fed his FEAR. And because there was no way of knowing what was next, the rifle on Viney's back drew the most hideous of pictures in his mind.

They had been walking and climbing right along with the morning sun. There were a few birds in song or in flight, but mostly Thomas noticed the trees losing their colored leaves in the wind. Woman and boy crossed grassy valley floors and climbed hills. They trudged up rocky slopes, and for a time, Thomas felt lost. Viney had a definite direction that she was headed in, for she quickly found the crossing log over the swift mountain stream in front of him.

Once on the other side, she stopped, put down everything but the rifle, and began barking orders. "This he'a is yer marker," she was piling up stones. "At sundown ye best be a sittin' right chere or I'm leavin' ye fer the buzzards." The food basket was thumped down on the biggest rock in the pile. "Boy, foller me." He did. Just over a small grassy knoll was the most remarkable landscape! She interrupted his awestruck wondering, "Fill 'em sacks. Won't bother me none ta leave ye here, but he ..." Viney mumbled on and headed away from him into the wilderness.

Thomas was stunned by the scenery and by Viney's cruel mumbling, but at last, he could finally breathe. He drank in the landscape. It was an old homestead with a few patches of fenced-in grass. He was standing in a grove of walnut trees. A shell of a house was pressed into the hillside with its chimney half-up and half-down. The logs were still trying to make a stand in the front, but the wind and rain had long since beaten out the chinking and ripped at its roof. He could still see the doorframe. The door tried to stand guard but lay on its side—injured.

Those magnificent walnut trees stood in a row, their fruit proudly spread on the grassy floor—like an offering. He felt as if the walnut trees were greeting him, and they had been so lonely for so long. *It t'would be rude not ta gather thur gift.* Thomas was grateful, for this time he wasn't going to have to work so hard. He was truly grateful for the change in scenery, but mostly he was grateful that FEAR was gone— for now.

He was thankful for not being locked in the room, that he could hear new sounds, see new sights, and he was bursting with thankfulness for the opportunity to think … OUTLOUD!

"Glory be!" He was shouting. "Now nobody's hangin' round ta tell me to hesh up. They's no one round ta keer what I do." His voice was echoing off the hills. The alone feeling was disappearing fast. "I'll jest take my time fillin' 'em sacks. I'm gonna poke 'round that chimley some, too. Might be sump'in I need." The usually cautious Thomas had given himself over to adventure.

He literally hopped and skipped and jumped his way over to that falling down homestead. Honest excitement, minus the FEAR, filled his chest. Without much trouble, his imagination filled in the blanks. As quickly as a question popped up, he was feeding it answers. "They was a tall strong Daddy, and a kind, gentle Mama. He was a farmer, and she was a real cook." He stepped through the door's opening and turned his face toward that fireplace. To him, it looked almost like a cave. "Must a been hur from olden days," he thought as his eyes were adjusting to the light, "Ya could stand two or three youngin's in thar."

And he was just about to stand inside that fireplace himself when he was clobbered by a mass of cobwebs. Instead, he sat down on the old wood box next to it.

Thomas was startled but undaunted. He quickly found a stick close by, removed the webs he could see, and swung at the "in case" ones. As he looked through to the opposite end of the home, he could make out the outlines of broken furniture. Carefully and slowly, he stepped forward not wanting to disturb a thing. "Some a the thangs was precious. 'Speshly ta her. Sure she cried buckets when they had ta go." He ran his hand across a lame table. "Broke 'em up pretty bad, I reckon. Maybe the crops didn't make it … maybe they all got sick … like Mama." He made his way respectfully back to the wood box and sat quietly for some time. *Whar ther' any chil'ren at 'his home?* He was truthfully picturing his own family. His heart made the images real. Ralph reading on the floor by the fire, Baby Toy climbing and crawling all over him, Brooks and Margaret chasing each other around the table. And Mama whistling while she fixed food. *Her beans and cornbread were the best.* But they didn't always have the beans. Sometimes it was just the bread. And not much of that.

His heart and head couldn't take anymore remembering. He jerked himself up, wiping the tears from his cheeks, "Wonder what's in 'his hur box?" When he found out, he was disappointed: "Sticks, (humf) might a knowd." The sun was straight overhead but it was his stomach that told the real time. Lickety-split, Thomas was out the door, through the walnut grove, and reaching for the basket. The menu was of little consequence. Viney's cooking was always boring, but hunger made it go down in spite of her carelessness.

He was engrossed in gathering the nuts when he noticed his filthy hands. "I'd best get ta the brook and warsh up. Besides, I'm thirsty." While sprawled out on his stomach, he scrubbed his hands in the running water. "Cold water don't always work on dirt. Works fine an' dandy fer thirst, though." The cold water gave him goosebumps inside and out.

And then carried on the cool wind, from somewhere upstream came a most hair-raising sound. *Was that a woman's scream?* No. Thomas knew that sound and immediately knew his life was in danger. Only one kind of animal made that exact sound. It was his limbs that were temporarily paralyzed with FEAR, yet somehow, he forced his eyes to search for the animal's whereabouts. Along the opposite side of the bank was the clear evidence—panther tracks.

A dangerous she-cat was on the hunt. Thomas would not stay in the open long enough to be her next victim, for when he found his legs, they carried him up the nearest tree. He shimmied high up into the sycamore tree. Unusual strength was in his arms and legs. He placed confidence in his quick reasoning and reflexes. The last time he heard a panther's scream, he was gathering wood with his brothers. The scene was playing in his mind with a realness that got caught in his throat. Together, he and his brothers had been in the woods, like he was today, gathering kindling for the morning fires. Mama had sent her little men out so that she could sweep the dirt floor of the cabin. Once the baby was resting and the boys had eaten, off they went. They had their arms full in no time, and it seemed odd that Ross was still in a hurry. The scream shook them, soundly. Thomas had noticed that both his brothers had been a little jumpy and worried all morning long. At the sound of that scream, Ross threw down his armload and grabbed him by the shoulders. "Do ev'r thin' I tells ye. Put down the wood, take off yer shirt." Ross was filling Ralph's hands with his own wood bundle and then tied the second bundle on Ralph's back. "I'm gonna tie Brooks on my back 'cause we gotta run fer our lives."

Ross clutched a long stick he had found for protection in one hand and took Thomas by the other hand. With Brooks tied on, Brooks' hands clasped tightly around Ross's neck, Ross and Thomas ran. Boy, did they did run. Ross insisted to Thomas, "Don't look 'round, just run. I spied her tracks back at the wood's edge. Forgive me for not goin' back home." Ross saved their lives, all right. That day, Thomas had seen the panther tracks too.

This time, Thomas was certain that he could only get help from himself. *What do I do next?* Now that he was off the ground, he could try to catch his breath. *Them big, black cats can climb trees. Easy. They sleep in 'em. Even father was skeered of 'em droppin' down on top of 'em in the night. Viney's got the only rifle and whar is she? I cain't sit on them rocks to get et up. I ain't plumb stupid. And yun's can ferget them buzzards gittin' a chance.* He remembered his knife. It wasn't funny.

The only one could git a laugh out of a sight like 'is is Satan, hisse'f. And Clifton. It wouldn't do to cry. Silence was the only help coming.

That Cauldron was nigh unto overflowing now that SELFISHNESS had added both FEAR and HOPELESS DESPARATION—an eternal favorite ingredient of the Accuser.

Where was the bright sunshine that had been with him all day? Why were the clouds pressing down on that valley just when he needed illumination? Thomas tried not to pay attention to his FEAR, but he forced himself to remain focused on staying alive.

Without a sound and just as he FEARED, that she-cat appeared, not in a shadow but in power, making her dark presence known. With silent movements, she sauntered through the grove of trees, passing right under him. She lifted her nose and head skyward. Why was she lifting her head? Was he discovered? He covered his mouth to keep the screams inside. No one could possibly hear him anyway. He calmed himself because he could hear the branch under him shaking noisily. It would not do to give himself away—if he could help it.

A stronger wind swept down that hill, strong enough that some of the bare tree branches clacked together. Thomas began praying fervently in silence: *The Lord is my Shepherd, I shall not want. Oh, Mama how does the rest of h'it go? Even though I walk through the valley* ... He would not be able to keep the tears back. They were already flowing. He wiped his face on his shoulder, completely embarrassed. His mind was screaming, *He'p! He'p!* He felt downright silly when he had had to quote that Bible chapter for school. It had never been any help to him, but his Mama loved to hear it. His father had only laughed at him.

The she-cat was still there, but when Thomas looked again, there was something else. She was being watched from down-wind. Was it friend or foe? It had the coloring of his moccasins, but was bigger than a dog. It crept closer, silently moving up the hill in a crouched position. This was not a game, for sure. She was being hunted.

Thomas was riveted, and as the Hunter got closer, Thomas could see a bow and quiver grasped tightly in the Hunter's right hand. It was definitely a man, but he never looked Thomas's way. He stayed fixed on his prey, stalking her with great skill. His silence proved it. But how long had the man been there? Thomas studied the Hunter's features. His head was bare with his long black hair in braids. Thomas could see brown feathers fluttering at the ends of those braids. The Hunter was sprinting to hide behind a huge tree.

The black panther was headed for the tree where Thomas was dangerously perched. He was convinced that he had been discovered by the she-cat.

Desperate was his plight, but he had more to focus on than just the cat. She was now hidden from Thomas's view because of the breadth of the tree, but like a silent flash of light, the Indian's arrow had been released.

No sound was heard. The whole scene was played out without one detectable utterance. With ancient skill and prowess, the Hunter had killed. Yet there Thomas was, the sole witness to her black mass lying lifeless on a pillow of dry leaves. Without a sound, the Indian then slung the she-cat across his shoulders and was making deliberate haste away from Thomas. Like a puff of smoke, he was gone—undetectable as he had intended.

This whole day was too hard to believe! Thomas blinked repeatedly trying to make sure he had seen what he had seen. Finally he remembered to breathe again, and as he scrambled down the tree, he looked for signs. He dropped to the ground, scouting with his eyes for any evidence of others. Convinced that he was alone, he crept in the direction where the kill had been. He moved forward being careful not to disturb the leaves, for he was earnestly in search of any proof that all this had happened.

His curiosity would not be served for the shadows of clouds and an increasing cool wind brought an uneasy feeling to the woods reminding Thomas that darkness would soon be settling in. With a shiver and a shout, Thomas declared, "I ain't gonna to be left behine." It was his imagination which forced his body to get busy. "Who knows what else is lurkin' bout?" He began to drag the black walnuts bags to Viney's marker. He felt rich and smart for every bag was full, and a generous amount was left for the critters. Thomas thanked the walnut trees for their gift. "I wonder if'n they know I thanked 'em?" The real question was how were two people going to carry all of those heavy bags back to the house?

8

Thomas had completed his chore. Viney would find him ready and waiting with the bags full of black walnuts. He had used the she-cat excitement to drag all those bags to the agreed meeting place at the rock. He didn't have the empty bags to protect him now from the night air. A shiver or two occasionally traveled down his spine as he waited.

He felt rich, somehow, with all those bags of black walnuts he had gathered. But the knowledge that the walnuts were never going to be his, nor would he likely benefit from their harvest, did not sting in the least. He would never be able to forget the day's events. All of those memories belonged solely to him. TIME could never take them from him. Today was his special memory. As the sun was setting, the adults came …

Clifton was driving the mules with Viney beside him on the wagon seat. The wagon bed was overflowing with hay. But the hay made a thumping sort of noise as it came up the hill. It was Viney that helped Thomas heave the bags of black walnuts into the wagon bed. After they were fininshed, she said, "Boy, you set down in that co'ner. Mind yer se'f."

He was past tired and nearer exhaustion, so "mindin' his se'f" was not difficult. *I'm gonna close my eyes an' sleep. If'n they need me, they'll holler.* The wind had blown the clouds away while Thomas and Viney loaded the walnuts, revealing the early night sky. So many things had happened that day; he heartily wished for chalk and slate. *Come to think of it, I never see'd Clifton or Viney readin' or writin', never! They's always workin' or watchin' me. Or whisperin'. Mama used ta make me copy my lessons. An' Holy Scriptures. The Indians write in picture 'words.'* It was much easier to keep his eyes closed and make the pictures re-appear than to believe he could have written them down. *Besides, slates break and nobody can take a remembrance from nobody.*

The road they traveled on was old and overgrown with grass, making the wagon rock back and forth. Thomas squirmed to make his small body nestle into the hay to keep from being miserably rattled. With his head resting on a sack of nuts, face open to the starry sky, Thomas noticed the Man in the Moon was full-faced and nodding to him like a long-lost friend. He wished once again that he could share his adventure with a REAL someone.

That old tattered piece of a quilt was all he had to shield him from the cold night wind. *Somehow, I gotta get me a hat. Maybe Clifton 'll go 'coon huntin an' I can work extree ta git the hide. Sure would he'p me keep from shiverin' all the time.*

The rocking of the contents in the wagon continued. Thomas noticed just how tired he really was after climbing trees, and being bent over for hours so to benefit others. A full moon filled the night sky and brightened everything. It was his usual pattern to be wide awake on such a night—but not this night. The leafless trees whispered their presence and bent forward seemingly just to watch him roll along this abandoned road. Thomas could detect the changing terrain, and he could sense that the incline of this road was at times steep. It felt a little like when he used to play on the swing in the schoolyard. That sensation made his thoughts wander: *Some of the times I used ta close my eyes when it was slowin' down. I never got two turns together, like 'em Blackberry Cove boys. Those Redmond brothers was always fightin' an' lovin' trouble. And the paddle ...* In mid-thought, Thomas fell sound asleep.

His sleep wasn't long in duration, but to his young limbs, it was as if he had slept for days. The wagon motion was like being rocked in Mama's chair after he had washed or hurt himself. The warmth of the hay and the old quilt comforted him. Even at the home cabin, comfort was certainly a luxury—with all the little ones running about and chores occupying Mama constantly. Mama was always thinking of "fun." The "fun" was certainly a disguise for helping her with chores. Most of the "games" they played were necessary. The children's father was unpredictable, leaving the responsibility to Mama. Even Thomas knew from experience not to depend on his father.

Thomas hated surprises. His father was full of the dreaded kind of surprises—the kind that came at a high price. A confusion of scenes was crossing Thomas' mind as he drifted in and out of sleep. *Was that a scream from the black cat? I can't see anythang.* He shifted his body and then tried to rest again. *No, that scream was Mama's.* Some of the surprises he remembered were cuts and bruises on her beautiful face. He got used to seeing her wear her hair down to hide the results of father's gifts. How many times had she received "a gift" that was really meant for Thomas or one of his brothers?

And then he remembered the telltale sign of impending doom. Thomas's guts were flipping and flopping as the wagon advanced toward the house.

I don't feel so good. An' that smell is awful. I never wanna smell that again. He was miserable. *I know that smell. I knowd it from somewhar dark.* Thomas was half-awake wondering why this smell was familiar. He was quickly breaking out in a cold sweat. Why was his shoulder wet? His thoughts were darting all over the place. *Is it rain? Nope. My leg is damp, too. What is this?* He was fully awake, now. Thomas investigated the noisy lumps beneath the hay where he was lying. *Corn liquor!* He clamped his thin lips together. *Trouble all 'round. How ignernt! All this mystery solved in the worst way. More truth!* Fury swept through him with such force his fists immediately were clenched and his jaw painfully set. *I been used! Cain't git fur enough away from this mean, hateful, wicked pizen. Ain't this a fine kettle a fish? Now what'll I do?* But, he wasn't going to get a choice, for out of the woods came … lanterns … and people.

9

Apparently Clifton had pulled off the road to hide amongst the trees. A small cluster of firefly-like beings kept their distance for the time being. Though there was a full moon, Thomas felt the darkness. The scene unfolded before him. One lantern went out, and one person moved towards Clifton. Evil Viney's face scowled down at him. There would be no misunderstanding this familiar look. He knew silence was his savior. He would have to behave naturally and calmly in order to save his hide.

For every face, Clifton handed off two, sometimes three jugs. Viney took coins. It was the strangest exchange: grown-ups met in secret and didn't say a single word. Then they slithered away off into the dark, one-by-one. Thomas hadn't moved, hadn't talked, and had not dared even cast one look at the faces. And he hadn't ever in his wildest of dreams expected this adventure. In no time flat, Viney rearranged the sacks and hay and planted herself back up on the wagon seat. The mules walked on. To the house. Where nothing changed.

Those two adults acted as if the events were nothing new. Out of the side of Thomas's view, he could not help but notice a moss-covered formation of rocks that had marked this strange encounter. Even more strange were the words that jumped forward from memories. *Rocks are dead. They have nothin' livin' inside 'em. They don't have feelin's. They don't get hungry or tired or thirsty and they cain't move by themse'ves. Teacher was right! DEAD.*

What a dark, dark night! Thomas's soul was heavy with pain. His heart hurt deep inside somewhere.

In the light of the full moon, there was a strategic gathering, and both the old and the new players were in attendance. HOPELESS DESPAIR was bragging to

ABANDONMENT of its recent accomplishments. To the players whose assignments were just beginning, The Accuser was shouting out the strategies around the bonfire as ABUSE took its turn stirring the thick black brew. During this celebration, the Cauldron of life was boiling and brewing with excitement because of the endless possibilities of new ingredients. REJECTION made sure to keep the fire hot so that the stench of HUNGER and LONELINESS would overtake the air that Thomas breathed in.

There was no mistaking the song SORROW played on its familiar instrument. All the while, DRUNKEN SPIRITS laughed eerily and uncontrollably at the sequence of events unfolding. NEGLECT was checking off items on the list of Thomas's life, congratulating everyone on having carried out a perfect plan of MISERY ... to the letter.

A broken wagon path. A broken respite. A broken peace of mind. A broken promise of a "room" ... that was actually a place of slavery. It wasn't over yet. More was to be revealed besides the corn liquor and Clifton's use of Thomas. "Boy, them jugs is goin' in yer room along with 'em walnuts. Now, git busy." Clifton placed a lantern in the room revealing their master plan. This "room" was never purposed to shelter and comfort a seven-year-old boy who just lost his mother. No, Clifton and Viney would never have allowed the room to be his personal space. They had from the beginning been planning instead to give comfort to little brown jugs of hatefulness and cruelty, and the proof was right before his eyes. It would never have occurred to them to ask Thomas if he needed anything or to ask if he was tired, discouraged, or lonely for his brothers or sister. All of these facts stabbed and slashed at Thomas's soul.

The Cauldron's brew was boiling over its edges and creeping right toward Thomas. He was standing in its deadly poisonous path.

Clifton and Viney's world revolved around … POISION! The evidence was overwhelming. Thomas had not one thing to call his own and not one person looking out for him. They even removed his straw bed, which proved their plan was working.

Thomas loaded the jugs that Viney handed him into that room. It looked small now. Had he not been so scared and mad, he would have counted every last one of them. This counting could have been the best sort of bookkeeping for all his hard work and unjustified beatings. They expected way too much of this seven-year-old boy. *Them mules get more than I do.*

Nothing was respected. Clifton came to wait outside the door to march Thomas to the next insult. "Sleep in the kitchen, boy." Thomas felt that he had more than earned the right to sleep on his own bed in that room! He checked himself quickly. Clifton's cold stare was like a door slamming in his face, making it perfectly ridiculous to give voice to his needs or preferences. Thomas put one foot in front of the other, following his nightly routine to the outhouse.

Clifton was waiting in the yard. When the two of them met again, he spoke his final two sentences of the night. "Boy, no matter what ye hear, don't ye dare come outta that kitchen. Ye make triple sure ye keep quiet or I'll fix it whar ye do—forever!" Clifton held a tight grip on the back of Thomas's neck as he forced the boy to make an oath. Then, Clifton took his giant hand and shoved Thomas into the dark shadows. Crawling under the table was natural and instinctive for Thomas. The sound of Clifton's boots moving toward the back of the house confirmed to Thomas "danger" was going to bed. Thomas stayed right where he was under the table. He was too cold to undress and too tired to look around for a better place to lay his head. But MERCY showed up that night, for somehow the quilt and ticking was under the table along with him.

Thomas knew the hour was late, but he was overwhelmed with the day's events. He found it hard to convince himself that all this had happened in one day. *Time never makes sense. I know I git up, eat, work, warsh, then sleep. That's a day. How long have they been workin' on that corn liquor? And by gum, whar did all them jugs come from? I never seed 'em before. I better start payin' attention. They must'a bin stored wherever they made their mash. I pray they don't make me do none a that corn liquor business.*

His thoughts ran to the old homestead. And Mama. Thomas couldn't help himself as he was now having to camp out under a kitchen table just to survive. *Mama loved the kitchen and the garden patch. She worked hard ever' day. 'Til she couldn't use her legs or her hands. Viney works all the time, and her hands are ugly, dry, and cracked. Mama's were tough but soft and gentle. Wicked Viney never cleans nut'in—and her skirts and aprons and petticoats stay caked in mud. Mama only owned two skirts—one dark and one brown calico. But they was clean. She always took care of the thangs she had. Even her apurns got pretty patches.*

It occurred to Thomas that Viney liked dirt—and the jugs. *Them dirty-brown jugs are her creations. Ever' last one of 'em.* He knew it was true. All her actions confirmed it. Another mystery solved …

10

Someone was clanking lids on the cook stove. Thomas's eyes popped open, and he slowly turned over onto his back. When he looked up, he realized that he was somewhere else. And then the previous day's events flooded into view. He had slept under the kitchen table. But who was making all that racket? With an ever-so-silent turning of his head, he recognized Viney's petticoat.

Should I move or jest be still? He knew his position in this life had not changed one bit, but he so hoped to be left alone for a spell. He needed to establish his plan for handling all that new information from the day before. He did not want to get caught again "not knowin."

Viney continued her banging and grunting to the point of distraction. "Boy, I need some water. Ye know whar the bucket is. I need my coffee!" She had remembered that the "boy" was handy. He obliged. But first he took care of his morning routine.

I won't have the same chores. There's a change comin' in the wind. It smells like snow. Ralph and Ross and Margaret and I used ta have ta get fresh hay for the beds and put new hay in the chicken coop before the first snow. I bet Viney don't make no fuss about the straw. All she cares about is them jugs, and I already took care a them precious thangs. Clifton won't be short of idees for chores even if he ain't 'round much.

Viney was now screaming for the water, and Thomas was quick to fill two buckets and get them to her. He wasn't in the door two seconds when she started in on him. She plopped down an empty tin cup and small plate with a boiled egg on it. "Eat quick. Thar's a heavy snow a commin' and ye got plenty a wood ta split 'n' stack. Yer main werry is not ta let the fire go out in the stove. You'll catch hell-fire if'n you do. I'm gonna work on this he'a venison stew. It'll be you eat'n on it, so you jest fetch me some taters from the root cellar. And some carrots if'n they's any left. Boy, 'ere ye hearin' me? Answer me, did ye get all I said?"

Viney was standing with one hand on her hip and the other held her tin cup, apparently waiting for the coffee to boil. "Yes'm, I heard ye."

Thomas gulped down some water and then reached under the table for the quilt. He needed a hat. He needed a coat. What he had was a used-up, left-over scrap of a quilt. He threw it around his shoulders and busted the kitchen door open. Once he was around the corner out of sight, he tied it around his waist. He had found the long string of leather in the bed of the wagon last night. He secretly slipped it into his pocket, praying they wouldn't see. Truly, it was his only reward for all the work he had done. *Better not make a fuss 'bout the cold! Might get this leather cord noticed. Clifton or Viney probably make quick use of hit. I cain't split wood and keep my quilt on at the same time! An' I ain't up ta no beatin' today.*

Thomas was in and out of that root cellar in a wink. His re-entrance this time was more respectful. He didn't want any trouble. Placing the vegetables on the table, Thomas tried to encourage himself for the work ahead. But his heart was not in it. There was no one to share the experience with. *Wonder what Brooks and Toy are doing today?* He trudged through the dead grass to the chopping log. *I hope Margaret and the boys are warm. Mama baked our taters on cold days.* Without thinking about it, Thomas began to sing while he was splitting the wood.

> "Hmm hmm hmm hmm (whack)
> hmm hmm hmm hmm (whack)
>
> Bill Grogan's goat (chop) was feelin' fine (whack)
> Ate three red shirts (chop) from off the line.
> Bill took a stick (whack) gave him a whack!
> And tied him to the railroad track ..."

He bent over to stack the logs.

"The whistle blew the train grew nigh,
   Bill Grogan's goat was doomed to die …"

He returned to the splitting log.

"But with a cough (chop) of awful pain (whack)
   Coughed up the shirts (chop) and flagged the train!"

It was time to check the fire in the stove. With his arms full of wood, he struggled to open the door. *I'll have ta put this load down and prop the door open with sump'in. But what?* He remembered seeing a rather large rock at the corner of the house. Thomas propped the door open and went back after the wood. Viney was finished with the stew and hollered for more water. Out the door, to the well, draw the water, in the door, out the door, back to the wood pile, to the house with his arms loaded again, get the rock, prop open the door, take the wood in, stack it beside the wood box, out the door, shut the door, back to the wood pile. More splitting and stacking. Alone.

Time to check the fire. One foot in front of the other.

He was perfectly content with the day's accomplishments. He never let the fire go out. Not even close. Viney was true to her word. She made the stew, and all there was to eat was the venison stew. Viney had disappeared from the kitchen before lunchtime, but not before she managed to reassure herself that Thomas knew his boundaries. When he had finished with the hauling of the last bucket of water for the day, he was to shut himself into the kitchen. All day Clifton remained absent.

Just as the sun was setting, Thomas could hear the angry boots approaching.

He scooted under the kitchen table once again. Clifton reminded Thomas to stay inside no matter what. Now Thomas was left alone with only a lantern on top of the table. Outside, a lonely cold wind was blowing, and it made a draft under the door. In the yard, all of the tree limbs clacking together sounded to Thomas like music—the kind that could put you to sleep. So after Thomas found something to stuff into the crack under the door, he took off his moccasins, untied the quilt from his waist, and proceeded to position himself to be sung to sleep.

Sleep would be just what he needed after his long day of working out-of-doors. With his eyes closed and the quilt pulled up to his chin, he began his prayer aloud, just as he did each night. "Thank you, God for keepin' the snow away til I got the chores done. My head and hands were perty cold without the snow. Bless Ralph, Brooks and Ross. And Margaret and Baby Toy. Do whatcha can fer 'em." He yawned again. "Help me think a how ta get a hat somehow, Lord. Thank ya. Good night. Amen."

The dreaming started right away. His dreams were vivid. The faces of his family popped in and out of focus. Pictures of himself carrying water and splitting wood came to his mind. Dreams of hunting the panther but finding instead footprints of a man's moccasin were swirling. In the next scene, he was walking back to the broken down homestead in the walnut grove, only everything was different. The house was standing strong and proud. A cow was in the field, and a dog was at the front door keeping guard over the place. He could hear laughter inside and could see smoke coming from its chimney. He could see calico curtains hanging at the windows, which were clean with the glass sparkling.

There was no mistaking the sound of the lid of a big iron stew pot being lifted, and someone banging a wooden spoon on its side. Thomas pictured himself resting on a rock, listening to the creek sing its song. And then all the sounds mixed together, awfully. The song was beginning to sound human-like. It was hurting his ears. A chorus of men's deep voices was coming on the wind but the words were jumbled up. *What is that noise?* He didn't want to wake up. He rolled over, hoping to make the noise disappear. It didn't. The voices got louder and closer, so close he popped his eyes open to investigate. *I musta been dreaming.*

//

There was only one window at the back of Viney's kitchen. It was covered in dirt and filth, and dressed in tattered, faded calico curtains attached to the top of the window with a string. Thomas could detect a change outside. The snow had come, as promised. And he was thoughtfully paying close attention to the white flakes on his way to the outhouse and the well. Thomas had seen snow before. The last time was when Mama bundled them all up and took them for a walk in the white covering. She seem so changed that time, changed from the hard working woman to a being with bigger concerns than chores.

Thomas remembered her words. "There's life goin' on, even when it's froze. God sends the snow a purpose, h'it's gonna make things grow in the spring. Don't ye jest love that small crunchin' sound under yer feet? Such a delightful sound … ye can only hear that very sound when hit snows." It was as if she whispered, "H'it's a peaceful blanket of rest. The Earth needs to get ready for new life. In Spring. God takes such good keer of His Earth. H'it's His mean purpose ta take keer of it and His children."

All of this memory was spent by the time he reached the well. The snow was coming down harder. *H'it's useless ta remember such thangs. They ain't no more good thangs. It's all a lie, now! An' I gotta keep my head straight. How long have I bin gone?* It wasn't really a question. It was more like a reminder of truth. He was shouting down the well and kicking it in between breaths. *No one, h'aint no one come ta see me. Hain't no one keered!*

Meanness and stark reality were now staring Thomas full in the face. Instantly there came the greatest and most natural of temptations. Would he become bitter and angry? *H'it's them lies that keep me ever on my guard an' them secrets what keeps thangs stirred up ta ruin me.* He knew what a lie was. But the truth was much more painful that snowy day without

Mama. He set his mind, wiped his wet, cold cheeks, and toted the buckets of water back to the kitchen, still a little out of breath from the battle.

Viney didn't even look at him. He hung his head anyway to avoid her noticing his red nose and wet eyes. While stuffing the dry biscuit into his mouth, he could feel her scowl. He gulped the milk. He usually drank the rare white liquid slowly and purposefully. Viney was sending Thomas to the root cellar for more potatoes and a squash. What she was going to do with them was, of course, a secret. She was back to her love of secrets. She wouldn't dare let him in on any of them.

His orders came one at a time. Thomas felt that she didn't trust him or anyone. The truth was that he did not trust her. He could never. There was no "smarts" in trusting that mean face.

Viney reluctantly loaned Thomas a small lantern and a red kerchief, mumbling something about him falling down the cellar ladder. She had no confidence that he could carry a heavy basket and manage a lit lantern.

He stood still while she rained insults and warnings. Once he was free of her, he made his way quickly to the root cellar. He moved the snow from the cover over the root cellar with a kick and set the lantern down. With very little effort, he was confident that he was on sure footing on the ladder, so, he picked up the lantern and continued to descend.

He liked the cellar fine, but today he wanted to be near the fire. The root cellar wasn't very big or deep and not nearly as full as Mama's root cellar.

About half way down, Thomas smelled a smell he once had wished for. APPLES!! He nearly fell off the last two rungs. Once he was on the ground, he rubbed his curly head with joy. With the lantern safely beside the basket on a shelf, he jumped and whistled. But what was he to do? Viney had not given instructions to fetch any apples. His mouth was watering. Thomas reached for an apple as fast as that. And hid it in his clothes.

He almost forgot what he had come for. Thomas's mind was sharp and contemplating the new found truth. He thought to himself, *I gotta be smart 'bout thangs now! This hur is a treasure, but h'it's not gonna turn this into a day for "The Belt."* He pressed his lips together confirming his resolve. He smartly gathered the potatoes and the butternut squash in the kerchief, tied a knot, and put it on his arm. Then he picked up the lantern and proceeded to climb the short ladder. Once he was at ground level, he unburdened himself, being careful to close the door. Nothing must happen to his discovery.

He would have to risk being caught with the apple. But it would be worth it. He whispered this hope under his breath. "I'll save it fer tonight. When they've gone ta bed. God he'p me ta save 'is apple." He needed the help with this secret of his own.

Viney was not in the kitchen when he returned. He took a deep breath in, and let it out slowly. He had been successful. Thomas kept his thoughts straight. *I'll sit right c'here in 'is chair. I'll wait 'til she gits back, and I'll wait 'til she gives my next order.* But he would not have to wait long. She came in and sent him out … to "split wood and get some dry logs in afore they get too wet." He went quickly and was quickly reminded his need of a hat.

How can I get me a hat? Maybe they's one in the cellar. H'it's been bustin' with surprises today. Now the snow was released from the clouds in little showers. He hastened his stride with the knowledge that the wood would most certainly not wait and neither would Viney.

He had lost count after 10 loads. Every load was covered deep in Thomas's scheming of getting a hat. And with every load, his face and hands and head and ears were exposed to the freezing temperatures. The whole day had been a dark gray as it squeezed out the sun. The clouds had more than squeezed out snowflakes. It was too dark and the snow was now coming in heavy showers. *I best herry with my warsh water and git ta tha house.* He could carry two buckets at a time now. The day was certainly coming to its end. What a relief it was to finally sit down. Dinner had been carelessly prepared as usual, and Thomas had to serve himself. They had not left much for him anyway. He ate from the usual tin plate with all its dents, using the crude wooden spoon. His mind was not at all on the food or the dishes, but on what a wonderful treat he was going to have under the table. It was still his very own secret!

With no adults around, Thomas had a little freedom. He could put more wood in the stove and get himself warmed up. He could take all the time he wanted to wash himself. No one was going to boss him around about that! He could take the whole night to look at the stars if somebody would wash the filth off the panes. Never mind, the stars were covered over.

He took great pains with his moccasins. He had certain "feelin's" about those shoes. They meant protection from cold and miserable pain. They were also one of his finest accomplishments. They were his proof of making it to the next day. So it was with loving care that he took his little knife and removed the chunks of wet earth. He used his sweet voice in song to encourage himself as he took the hay from his ticking to stuff his shoes, helping them to dry out. He stole some grease from the crock on the kitchen shelf, when he was really brave, so that he could make sure they stayed soft and didn't crack.

Voices could be heard across the yard. The voices penetrated the kitchen door. This was not just Viney and Clifton bickering about chores. These voices forced Thomas under the table, in retreat. He looked around for another type of protection, for what was going on outside was violent. These voices belonged to men. But how many? And what were Clifton and Viney going to do with them?

He would not have to guess what was next, for Viney came stomping through the door, slammed the door, and went to the back of the house. Thomas could hear her bumping into furniture and cursing. He could hear her boots thumping their way back to the kitchen. She produced the rifle and clenched bullets in her left hand and thrust them into that infamous pocket. She moved forward to the door, but not without barking commands to Thomas.

"Stay thar! I mean business. Thar's hell a brakin' loose out chere. Stay right thar!" Slam went the door and BLAMM went the gun.

Thomas planted himself under that table tempted to cover his innocent eyes, but the door had bounced open from its violent touch from Viney. While under his fortress, Thomas lie flat on his stomach to watch the goin's on.

It was most likely Clifton he saw holding up an oil lantern in the shadows, but it was definitely Viney with the command of everyone's attention.

"Now git! Did ya heer me? I said git! Ya got what cha come fer." The men moved towards Clifton, but not before Viney lowered the gun and pulled back the hammer.

That distinctive sound forced all to turn on their heels and scatter into the dark. Viney shouted, "An' don't cha come back, lessin' yuns want a belly full—an I don' mean liquor!" Clifton patiently waited for her to move the barrel of the gun away from his direction so that he could move. Then he and Viney walked away from the house. There was only two places for them to go—to the barn or to the jugs.

Thomas's insides were shaking and his eyes were fixed on the two shadowy figures moving away. As he crawled on hands and knees to close the door, he felt exposed.

What if one of 'em men tries to git Clifton or Viney in their sleep? He hurried back to safety. *What if they have a gun? What if I git shot by mistake?* His imagination was getting the best of him. He shook himself soundly. *That's a 'nuff. They's too mean ta let anyone git that close—Viney can smell trouble. Nothin' gits by her!*

Mama was always there in times of TROUBLE. Father was TROUBLE! *I'm all I got.* FEAR and INSECURITY helped Thomas cry himself to sleep. The apple must wait. It deserved reverence. Not turmoil.

12

It was snowing when Thomas went to the outhouse and well the next morning. It felt different from the night before. Why was it different? *I do the same thang ever mornin'. Maybe snow does make thangs quiet and peaceful.* As Thomas drew the water, his peace was disturbed with an announcement. Thomas could hear the distinct sound of a turkey's call. The turkey was close by. And from the direction of the barn, Clifton came running. "Whar's the gun?" He was trying not to shout. Thomas of course did not know the answer. But Clifton slapped his face anyway.

He turned away from those giant hands just in time to avoid more pain. "Right chere, an here's the bag. Good luck!" Viney mysteriously appeared with Clifton's supplies. "I'm plumb tarred a venison … boy, hop to it. I need water fer the cookin' an' the warshin'." She twisted in her stiff skirts as she went inside where it was warmer. Thomas stayed outside where it was colder and where he started over, drawing more water and feeling convinced nothing could change—turkey or not.

Out in the barn, Thomas sat in the cold, on a log, plucking the turkeys clean. Clifton took one of them to the smoke house and put the other one on a spit over a fire. A fire Thomas had to watch. All day long. So the front of Thomas warmed first while snow and wind blew at his back until he couldn't take the shivering any longer. Then he turned around. He had to risk it. He had to be careful to make it look like he was continuously watching that fire. Clifton's threats never went unchecked. He made the best of the day's chores. He had no lunch. And he had cornbread and milk for supper. And he had to trudge through the deeper snow on his way to his evening ritual.

There were more "visitors" that evening. But Thomas went to bed as usual. The slap on his face was a reminder of his place in this life.

And so when he placed his little, cold, hungry, weary body in its place to rest, he began whispering a new prayer under his breath.

"God, I knowd I did nut'in' ta be slapped fer, and so does Clifton. He'll git his come-up-ins fur shur. I wanna talk to ya 'bout my hat. My head hurts fer thinkin' of how ta git it. So maybe while I'm sleepin' ya could tell me how! Bless Brooks, Ralph, Margret, and Toy. Ross an' me … Goodnight—Amen."

So many were the nights that repeated themselves. Some were a little more noisy than others. Thomas tried to sleep through them. The sounds were not interesting and usually resulted in Viney shouting her threats.

On a windy night, their voices did carry with volume and seemed to go on forever. That is, they carried on until daylight began peeking around and over those hills of Dark Ridge. One night before daylight, he could hear men's voices singing. The song was out of tune and the timing was off but the words were undeniable.

"What child is this who lay to rest on Mary's lap is sleepin' …"

Chris'mas? Was it time fer Chris'mas? How could it be time fer Chris'mas? When Thomas added up the events and seasons there could be no argument about the time. He was stunned. And stabbed through the heart.

"Whom angels greet with anthem sweet …
the babe, the son of Mary …"

He remembered Mama's words and some words from her big black Bible: "Chris'mas is bout fam'ly. Mary and Joseph were the ones chosen ta be the earthly fam'ly fer God's son, Jesus. Chris'mas day is Jesus' birthday. The birthday of the Savior of all the people that ever lived, and ever will live. 'Fer God so loved the world, that He gave His only begotten Son, that whosoever believeth in Him, shall not purrish but have everlastin' life.' The greatest gift ever given. The gift of life."

TIME was marching onward. But there was no hope, no love, no comfort this Christmas for Thomas. No gift, no celebration, no family, and no life. There was nothing new, except the new feeling of dread.

Thomas did dread facing tomorrow—alone. Of course, it had to be another day without Mama. He could not change that.

The Christmas wind blew. It blew across that Cauldron, causing its thick, ominous, choking vapor to lift. No one was there to prevent the wind from filling Thomas's nostrils. It meant to overpower Thomas. It was mocking him and tormenting his memories—his beautiful memories of love, protection, and hope. He was in the dark, swirling around and around in vicious black waters. Down, down, down—he was being pulled.

At the same time, in his dreams, his Mama's voice was calling him. "Thomas, I love you … most precious gift, life …"

The following dreaded morning, Clifton and Viney were in their usual state during daylight hours. Asleep. But Thomas was wide awake. He had not been able to sleep with the heavy heart in his chest, nor could he find a place of rest for the new burden was heavy on his shoulders. He quietly slipped out-of-doors. His head hung down in sorrow. He had no need to look up, besides he knew he could make this trek with his eyes closed. On he trudged to the well to leave the two buckets. On he went to the outhouse. His breath hung in the frozen air. On to the well, where he pulled up the bucket while his ears and cheeks and nose stung from the cold.

Two buckets full of water. Two buckets to carry back. Two hands to carry them. Two legs to carry him. Two feet pressing down on the cold earth. Thomas didn't really care how things looked. Yes, the sun was going to shine, but darkness was coming, too. It was usually a quick trip from well to kitchen, but Thomas was struggling with where to find the courage or strength to face reality.

The buckets felt so heavy today. He set them down. And then he sat down. *It's so quiet.* LONLINESS was befriending him. He looked around.

GRAY stared back at him. All the GRAY. GRAY house, GRAY windows, GRAY dirt, GRAY snow. But there was something not GRAY sticking out from under the corner of the house. Something furry and brown. With a black stripe. A COON! Thomas ran to find a long stick. "Best be keerful, he might be hurt. An' mean." He silently, carefully crept up to the ball of fur. It did not move. He steadied himself. And he studied its shape. It was flat. "I'll poke it ..." Nothing happened ... He moved the stick over it ... He gingerly slid the stick under it and held his breath as he lifted it.

Hallelulia!! It's a hat! One of 'em men left it behine when Viney skeerd 'em. MERRY CHRIS'MAS!! MERRY CHRIS'MAS!! He proudly dusted it off and placed it on his head in triumph. He was feeling like a new man. And with his new hat on his head, and a burden lifted off those little seven-year-old shoulders, he danced. And jumped. *An' while no body's lookin', I'm gonna get me two apples.*

He jumped his way to the cellar. He took care not to make too much noise. Discovery might mean DEATH. He was momentarily disappointed to find fewer apples and the thought occurred to him to hide a few in his own secret places. He promised himself out loud, "An' that is jest what I'm gonna do!" He finished hiding the secret apples, then grabbed two for his Christmas Dinner. Up the ladder he went, not fumbling at all for the light from the sun had been sufficient. Thomas silently replaced the cover over the cellar and fetched his buckets to the kitchen.

Viney would need her coffee. Clifton would need to be surly and cruel. Thomas would need to eat breakfast for now his stomach was yelling.

But their SELFISHNESS spoke loudest, and those two would not stir. While he waited, he looked around for something to help quiet the noise coming from his empty pit. Not much was found, and his precious apples were calling to him. But FEAR's voice was louder, reminding him of "The Belt." Thomas would have to be satisfied with old, dry turkey scraps. Christmas came, and then it ran away—running away from the DREAD and HOPELESSNESS.

13

A biting cold wind moved down the valley floor of Dark Ridge. It lingered and tortured Thomas for 10 days. With his little knife, he made a mark under the tabletop for every visit it made. And each night, the wind howled and moaned its way between the big cracks in the doors and windows of that house. During those days, he rushed through every outdoor chore, trying to keep his hands from freezing. His pants and shirt were too thin to sufficiently protect anyone, but they were all he had—they were all Clifton and Viney wanted him to have.

They actually didn't notice how thin his clothes were, didn't notice the coon hat that he had found, and they didn't notice the quilt that he also used as his coat. And they didn't notice that the food was the same old food. Beans, cornbread, maybe one egg, dry biscuits, and leather britches. Round and round, nothing new. Oh, occasionally it snowed, occasionally Viney cooked potatoes, occasionally Clifton chopped wood. Occasionally, rarely, Thomas was warm. But he was never NOT hungry.

During those scarce warm moments, Thomas thought about the home cabin. He remembered the happy times under the quilts, hiding from the cold. Mama would bake potatoes and put a little grease and salt on their skins. She would feed the children and then herself. The children's father wasn't there, but Thomas was sure his father was always warm and never hungry. That was not a lie.

Clifton was never hungry or cold. No matter what Viney cooked, he always got the first of it. And he always got as much of it as he wanted. He let both Thomas and Viney know when things weren't right by his standards. He was the one probably eating all the apples! His overalls looked solid and his coat thick and complete with buttons.

Clifton had two sets of longjohns. Both Clifton and Viney had leather gloves to work in and to protect their hands. And scarves to shield their necks and chests from the blowing winter winds. Clifton's boots were real thick leather.

Thomas was still very proud of his moccasins. And his leather string. And of course, he was deeply grateful that God had answered his prayer that Viney and Clifton wouldn't notice the hat that God had let him find and keep.

14

How short the daylight hours were, and yet, Thomas had lots of chores that had to get done outside in the light, along with drawing all the water they needed for their coffee and cooking. Clifton had also hauled some logs to the yard for Thomas to split. Thomas had to make the usual visits to the root cellar for vittles. He wondered if Clifton or Viney knew how low the potatoes were and if they knew that there were no more squash or leather britches left. Viney had already griped to Clifton, and anyone else listening, that the venison "is disappearin' right afore my eyes!" Clifton's response was always, "Go huntin' yersef! Yuns is the ones eatin' up the supplies."

One morning before daylight came over the hill, Clifton did take his gun and bag. Thomas did not know the plans of course, but it did shock him when Clifton returned home with a fist full of dead plants tied up with a string. It was the same day that Viney never got out of bed. Clifton boiled the coffee and the eggs for them to eat. It was he who ordered Thomas to fetch more water and not to mess around. On his return, Thomas placed the water pail on the floor. Seeing Clifton in the kitchen was strange. And so were the sounds. Pots and lids clanging together. Heavy boots making quick steps. There was also the unmistakeable miserable sound of a woman coughing in the back of the house. Thomas stayed out of harm's way. Without being told, he kept the fire going in the stove and the kettle filled with water.

Those dead plants were put in Viney's biggest black pan and covered with hot water. It steamed a big cloud and Clifton put its heavy lid over it and then carried the whole thing back toward the coughing sounds.

All day long, Clifton was going from the kitchen to the back toward the coughing, taking care not to spill the hot pot of steam. Three times he removed the dead plants, replaced the old water, and started a fresh brew with a new bunch of dead ones from the bundle. It reminded Thomas of the time Brooks and Toy got the coughs and Mama did the same routine. *She looked plumb tarred that time. Clifton just looks plumb put out!* The coughing did not stop.

When darkness came, Clifton went outside. He left instructions for Thomas. "Stay in the kitchen. They's nothin' ta be done 'bout her." And so Thomas put a little more wood in the stove and scrounged around for something to eat.

There was a full moon that night which always made it hard for Thomas to go to sleep. He imagined taking long wagon rides on roads stretching and winding through beautiful orchards of apple trees. He tried to imagine the taste of apple butter, even though he had never had any. Mama said it was her favorite thing about apples. Thomas began his prayers whispering, "God, help Viney to quit coughin' an' bless me with some sleep. Take keer of Margaret and Ralph and Brooks and Toy. Ain't it close to Spring, yet? God bless me. And Ross. Good night, Amen." Now he was yawning.

The door swung open and a cold hand was gripping his ankle. Thomas was rubbing his eyes, clutching his quilt, and trying to focus on the huge form in front of him. It was Clifton. "I need ya out chere. We got cus'amers." He was dragging Thomas by the arm, with Thomas struggling to get control of his bare feet. "You stand in hur," Thomas was shoved into the "room" with the brown jugs. "I'll tell ya how many ta hand over an' you make a mark on the wall thar." Clifton showed Thomas a real pencil tied to a long string. "Don't ya git any idees. I don't need ya ta do nut'in else till I says so." Thomas was more afraid of Clifton than he was of being out in the cold without his hat or moccasins. Good thing he had held on to the quilt.

Clifton was waiting under the big oak tree right outside the door to the room. The same tree that had had the deer dangling from its huge limbs. "The Belt" was also on Clifton and tied to it was the bag. But Thomas did not see hide nor hair of the gun.

The two were just waiting. Clifton on "cus'amers" and Thomas on handling the jugs and making the marks. They did not have to wait long. The first customer was tall and skinny. He gave his coins to Clifton and Clifton told Thomas to "mark down two jugs." It would be the first time Thomas had ever touched a real pencil. With careful attention, he made the marks in the right place. With the same careful attention, he handed over one jug and then the other. The customer slunk back into the dark, and Clifton moved back under the oak. Thomas was now aware that more customers lurked around in the woods.

But there was something not right about things. It was not easy to see their faces, but Thomas did detect more than two men moving through the yard and advancing toward the oak tree. They struck up a friendly conversation with Clifton—but something was not right. Thomas was frightened.

He thought that he could hear a low growl faintly moving through the little trees behind the well. He was second-guessing himself. *It was just the wind.* He shifted his focus back to the oak tree. Out of the corner of his eye, he noticed that one of the customers was backing up, moving away from Clifton. Thomas flattened himself against the wall, allowing himself access to the opening so he could spy. His attentiveness paid off. Those keen young eyes could not be fooled!

There were more than three men. He could just make out the form of an animal—one large enough to ride on but it was not a pony.

It was a huge dog, whose fur was dark and shaggy. Its whole body was straining to free itself from the rope tightly gripped by its master. The dog was growling deep in its throat and its focus was on Clifton.

The two customers violently grabbed Clifton's arms when the third one shouted, "NOW!" Clifton was caught in the middle of the two men with the third searching his pockets and swearing at him. "Whar's the money? Don't git no foolish idees." But, before anyone could find the coins, Clifton broke loose and swung his giant fists towards their stomachs. The third man jumped on his back but Clifton slung him off. And then the dog strained forward, almost running and loudly barking, with its master yelling, "Tear 'im up, Bear! Tear 'im up, I sayed!"

No one but Clifton knew Thomas's actual size, but he felt small and defenseless. So, Thomas slipped out of the doorway and picked up a big rock. One for each hand. He pressed his back against the room's outside walls. Staying in the shadows was safe. He watched, gripped with fear as the dog was jumping and fighting to get loose from his master's grip. Clifton was still swinging and landing his fists and feet where it counted. Silently, the master let loose of the rope. Clifton naturally wheeled around looking for the next place to land his fists. Forward lunged the animal, going instinctually for Clifton's throat. Thomas made his rock fly.

The dog was in mid-air, with Clifton staring in disbelief. He stepped backwards, bracing himself and quickly thrusting his forearms up to shield himself. The rock struck expertly and squarely on the side of the dog's huge head. The rock had found its mark all right, for the animal lay silenced at Clifton's feet.

All three of the men jumped to attention and with frantic haste ran back to the dark mountains from which they came. The master was running, looking back over his shoulder, waiting for the dog to catch up. Clifton was standing, looking down at the dog. He kicked the animal in its side. No movement. Not even a whimper. "Boy, whar 'ere ya?" He didn't wait for Thomas's reply. "You stay in that room. I'm gonna stand watch from he'a."

Thomas could see Clifton shifting his coat and picking up his hat from the ground. He placed it back on his head, and Thomas was prompted to look for the quilt.

With the gang of men gone and the threatening dog put down, the welcomed opportunity came for both Thomas and Clifton to breathe and relax for a moment.

The stars were out, and the quiet went uninterrupted for some time. More cus'amers came. Clifton and Thomas picked up where they left off. Jugs and money and marks on the wall. They came and went. Clifton was not friendly with anyone. They were "cus'amers" to him.

Some of them were women who brought empty jugs to exchange for full jugs of "pizen." The brown jugs contained poison that kills families. His mind was working on making sense of the senseless occupation with corn liquor.

Pizen, that's its name ... snatches away happy times and swaps 'em with miz'ry. And turns fathers into mean dogs. And churns up devilment. Some old memories still haunted Thomas. *Why don't they jest go home ta they's chil'ren an' love 'em, not love 'em jugs? Why cain't they jest go home and stay thar! I cain't go home. I ain't got no home.* Thomas wiped his nose on the back of his quilt sleeve.

The night was over when Clifton crossed the way and counted the jugs remaining in the room. Thomas was weary, cold, and numb. Clifton locked the door, and both of them shuffled their way to the kitchen. Thomas almost fell onto his pallet under the kitchen table. Clifton's boots scooted on the wood planks all the way to the back of the house. All the sounds were fading, and sleep was covering the boy.

15

The sun stayed up in the sky longer. A few more birds made their way across the tree tops and chirped and tweeted. But it was still cold at night, and Thomas began to grow weary of his life. The path beneath him was unchanged. He still rose each day to fetch two buckets of water, went to the outhouse, and returned to tasteless food and pointless repetition. The two adults were still keeping their secrets and watching him faithfully. Thomas had long since eaten all his secrets.

Clifton never mentioned that night under the oak tree. The brown jugs were fewer in number, but only the occasional rain reduced the time they had to spend watching for customers. Viney and Clifton both continued to use Thomas to do whatever work they wanted him to do, refusing to change how they saw him.

Thomas's stature was small. He looked more like a six-year-old than a boy of almost eight. He had two loose teeth. His frame was light and thin. His eyes had not changed from their pale blue color. But Thomas could see more than enough with those young eyes, and he could reason well with his experienced mind. TIME had not changed his position, nor was he in a position to call out to TIME for help.

Thomas knew for certain nothing and no one could stop the Earth from changing its clothes. TIME was marching on, and the seasons were about to change. There were already signs of green life on the trees and the hills.

The days became warmer, and the creeks and well were full of water from the melted snows up-hill. Already, behind the barn, he had spied some daffodils blooming—a sure sign of spring. And planting was to come soon too.

Unlike the Earth that changed itself, Thomas could not change his clothes, for the worn-thin shirt and pants that he wore everyday were the only clothes he had. But his body had changed some. He was a little taller. How did he know this? His pants were shorter, and his shirt could not tuck in. And the quilt didn't always cooperate at night. His hair was thin still, but it was longer. The curls were still there, often refusing to cooperate with him when he washed. His little knife was working on a solution to this frustration. He was determined to fashion a comb. How hard could it be?

His moccasins needed patching, but there was nothing to patch with. Clifton was not in a hunting mood and that was that. Viney kept her fabric scraps hidden. Well, Thomas couldn't find any of them in the kitchen, at least. There would be no obvious benefit to asking for the flour sacks when they were emptied either. She hid those from herself and stayed in a tizzy because of it. She had already accused Thomas of stealing them. There was no benefit in arguing with her. She had proven herself mean and spiteful. He willingly turned the kitchen upside down searching for the lost sacks. Unsatisfied with the results, she turned on Clifton, who owned up to using them. Viney was silent. Thomas did not know what to think about a silent Viney. Strange.

Clifton was not pleasant to be around, and he was downright dangerous when he was aggravated, which was pretty much all the time. He even cussed at the mules for being mules. Chores seemed to unravel Clifton. But they must be done. He made this announcement to Thomas one morning with a kick under the table. "Gotta hitch them mules to the plow. I'll meet cha in the field boy." Clifton's impatience insured that Thomas would have just enough time to relieve himself, wash, and fetch Viney's water. But there wouldn't be any wisdom in waiting for food. Better to be hungry than risk a beating.

Farmers need to turn the soil before the last winter's snow so that it can be enriched. Clifton's cornfields yielded plenty last harvest; they had a bumper crop for sure. He had his formula for success, and there would be no detours allowed. He was just the sort of man not to let anything or anyone get in his way. It would not be tolerated.

The wind was pushing at Thomas's back and was doing its best to try to remove his 'coon skin hat from the curly hair on his head. He tied the quilt on tighter and ran with his hand on his hat to the field. He found Clifton already behind the plow with the mules trying to oblige. They began the harvest, passing the first cut of the ground with ease. They made the second and third pass with only two stops for rocks and roots. The moccasins made keeping pace difficult, but Thomas didn't want Clifton to suspect a thing, so he journeyed on. The mules found their plowing rthym. Man and boy followed behind. Thomas continued to watch for rocks, roots, and trouble.

Viney came with the basket and hot coffee. She waited patiently for Clifton, and then in sharp contrast, impatiently gave Thomas his warning. Away went Viney with the basket of corn, and on walked the mules, with the earth breaking beneath their hooves and feet.

The only sounds occupying the air were the jingling of the plow's chains and Thomas humming under his breath—that was until a metal scraping noise halted the entire group. Clifton pulled back on the reins. He investigated the plow. The man was on all fours looking intensely at the implement. Out came a string of familiar curse words, which always made Thomas shrink. "Ye broke it! Blame it! Snapped it in two! You was 'pose to be watchin' but NAW!! ... you was lolly-gaggin. You good-fer-nothin' ..." Those hands were reaching for him and there would be no use in running. He was too close.

"I was watchin'," he defended, "an' besides, it was under the dirt!" Clifton grabbed him by the shoulders and squeezed. That man's face was full of hate and meanness, "Whad ch'a say? You ain't ta blame?" It was more than that man could absorb and his response to the boy was to jerk him up into the air and violently shake Thomas. "You'll pay, I'll make damn sure of it." While he was being shaken, one moccasin slid off his foot and then Clifton released him.

When Thomas's feet touched the ground, he ran. He ran and looked back over his shoulder. And he choked back fear and tears and ran, throwing off his other moccasin. He looked back, Clifton was left in the field to tend to the plow and the mules but he would be coming after him.

Where could he hide? There would be two adults searching for him in no time flat. But Clifton had to cool off sometime. How long would that take? Thomas ran to the room. Somehow, miraculously he found it unlocked, and it would make the perfect place for him to catch his breath. He was shaking so hard that his knees were banging together.

It didn't take long for the man to put away the tools and mules. And to walk over to the room with the brown jugs and the boy in it and LOCK IT! And laugh. "Ye can jest stay thar, all night. Maybe no food'll teach ya ta quit yer lyin' and sassin'. I bet cha'. An' when we git cus'amers, I'll be watchin' ya all night, a thinkin' on how to git that new plow blade outta yer hide."

Thomas had been holding his breath. But he could breathe now. It made no sense, but the closed and locked door gave him peace. He took his hat off, untied the quilt, and lay down on his back. He would have to face Clifton, and with that thought, his eyes closed tightly. He had spent all his energy, and he felt completely exhausted. Thomas rolled over onto his side, lay his head on top of his coon-skin cap, slipped the quilt over his hip and legs, and slept.

A heavy rain beat down on the land and drummed against the walls and the door. Thunder rolled around and around in the heavens. And then things quieted down. The room was losing light, and with its loss, would come the proof that darkness had to come.

Hunger woke Thomas. Up he sat, and realizing that he would have no dinner, he went right back to sleeping. The rain went right back to beating, and the thunder came rolling around. Wind that tore at the trees and the building sent rain under the door of the room. Thomas was getting wet, and the air was getting cooler. He began to get uncomfortable, noticing the change. A few flashes of light woke him and revealed the water that was being driven under the door. More water was coming down, and more water was coming in. "This storm's gonna keep all them cus'omers at home whar they belong." Thomas breathed a sigh of relief.

He was granted solitude to consider the meanings of the two events and the two rocks. He said quietly, "I h'aint never lied to narry a one of 'em. I h'aint sassed 'em an' always done what I bin tole. That rock was hid under the dirt an' the proof is … Clifton didn't see it neither. So there! He's got money of his own ta buy a new blade fer that plow. They's so much liquor 'round chere, he could buy a whole new one."

The injustice caused him to stand to his feet. Growing louder, Thomas continued, "I only done them good. An' Clifton knows hit. That dog smelt blood an' hit was Clifton's. Hit was my rock that struck it and saved his life. They's no lie in that!"

All that confessing and declaring would in no way alter the testimony of Clifton's hands. They had shaken Thomas—shaken him to the point of desperation. Again it was proven to him that those giant hands were connected to an unreasonable, cruel man—one who was driven by selfishness and hatred. Thomas shivered. Fear and dampness went through his clothes, past his skin, and penetrated him to the bone. He fell to his knees in a heap on the wet floor. "What hope is thar? I'm left here with no way ta escape." His little hands covered his face to drown out his sobbing. The howling wind repeated its visits and the storm picked up pace.

The gloomy miserable room helped keep Thomas's thoughts dark all through the night. The brown jugs laughed at the hopeless little boy trying to hide from reality.

The Cauldron was beyond restraint. Its thick, hateful concoction was boiling over the rim and running towards him, aiming to consume him. DESPAIR and ABUSE were ambitiously planning their celebration. The cold wind and rain were marking the obvious.

An eerie glow reached under the door. A man's voice shouted, "Thomas get out chere, now!" The voice was Clifton's, but it did not sound normal. The storm had been raging for hours and the drumming rain competed with the clashing of thunder. The door violently opened, and almost simultaneously, Thomas was cruely snatched up by those infamous giant hands and pitched outside to the soaked ground.

"That cow has bolted and I ain't a-gonna chase her no more! That's what yer here fer. All hell's broke loose an' dad-blame-it if'n I'd hunt fer my own se'f in this storm. 'Tis yern ta do that drinks the milk. I don't need it." Clifton was railing and justifying all the while he was standing dry inside Thomas's room.

The scene in front of him took him by surprise. Suddenly Clifton seemed hideous and disgusting, and Thomas realized something for the first time. That was enough! He had had enough. Thomas stood soaking wet from that cold rain, trying to gather his thoughts when the heavens cracked wide open with a bolt of lightning that split the biggest oak tree in the yard to its soul with enough illumination to set Thomas's feet to flight.

Past the outhouse and down the wagon path … he was running for his life. Thunder bellowed and echoed in his chest. There was no plan … just revelation. There were no shoes. Just feet searching for freedom's road. With every flash of lightening, he could visualize just enough to run a little further.

If I can get through the corn patch to the woods, then I can stop to breathe. I'll make him think I'm goin' after the cow. Thomas didn't know which had the loudest voice: the thunder, the lightening, or his thoughts.

Running in the darkness was a comfort just then. As he ran, his mind was thinking and acting for Thomas. He alone was the one making the plan. The lightning was so bright that he was blinded at times, but nonetheless, he was determined. "Gettin' hard to breathe, gotta make it look like I'm still sarchin' for the cow. Maybe just 10 more paces an' I'm deep enough into the woods to fool 'em." His confidence was growing. But the reality of his freedom could not be realized just yet. There was the current issue of surviving the natural storm and the impending fury of the "Clifton" storm.

Had it not been for the terrific lightening and him being blinded by the sideways blowing rain, Thomas could have been convinced this was all just a nightmare. But oh, it was real. Ahead of him was the tree line and … freedom. He just had to make it to a rock or something to hide behind and catch his breath. On and on he ran until he found his rock.

Down he went to his knees so as to camouflage himself. "I know he'll hear me tryin' to catch my breath. If'n a deer can be still right next to the Hunter, so can I!" He steeled himself. Surely Clifton would stick to his word about not looking for the cow.

More rain and lightning made the hiding place difficult, but nonetheless perfect, for Clifton would not be looking for the cow in this storm. Thomas had long since known that he had about the same value as an animal. Clifton and Viney had made great use of him during all the seasons. But it was raining freedom, and he had—for the first time in his young life—come face-to-face with a cleansing shower.

No matter how hard the downpour, Thomas had to be cleansed from the stench of NEGLECT and HOPELESSNESS. He was going to face those ominous mountains with vigor and life. HOPE was just over the next ridge.

There was such a river of HOPE streaming down the mountain before him. A song swelled up inside his chest, but it would necessarily have to be sung in silence. *God will he'p me, I know it!* And on he marched.

At this point, Thomas was farther than he had ever been. But it would not be far enough. He had to make sure Clifton and Viney would not be able to find him. This time he spoke outloud. "As long as hit rains, I best keep climbin'. I gotta git so fer from here." It was turning in to a climbing and sliding game for the rains were coming down in sheets, and the dead leaves left nothing to hold on to. He put one hand on a sapling, pulled himself forward, planted one foot deep as it would go, and repeated this. When he got to a flattened ridge, he ran, jumping over the rocks and fallen logs.

He wasn't going to look back. "They's nothin' to look to back thar! Hope is in front of me. I'm gonna keep runnin' 'til I have ta rest. An' I'm gonna rest when I wanna rest!" He didn't look back—not even once. That was his plan. *His plan.* What wonderful words! He stuck to the plan, resting only a few times, climbing ever higher and farther from the reach of those two cruel, violent, loveless beings.

All that hard work had made Thomas pretty strong. He could

definitely endure more climbing. Going up was better than down. Down felt wrong. It felt lifeless. He had had enough of that, too. Even though the sun was supposed to be moving up in the sky, its evidence was weak. The mountain was still shrouded in the heavy rain and strong winds. This plan—his plan—would have to depend on TIME, and Thomas knew it. It wouldn't work any other way. TIME was marching on; it always does.

Day turned into night, and the now eight-year-old boy picked a place of protection beneath a rock ledge. He rested his back against one of the rocks and waited for the rain to cease and for the daylight to burst forth with real encouragement. He rested, between peals of thunder and bursts of lightning.

Morning had come at last and the rain had slowed. The boy was wide eyed and thinking his plan through. *I'll look for chim'ley smoke. Might work ... might be one of them "cus'amers". Have ta chance hit. I h'aint tared, yet. I'll walk a spell an' think some more.*

He thought and walked and got rained on some more. It was not always a gentle rain. *Won't have ta warsh. An' my clothes are clean, ta boot!* He would have to keep taking one step at a time. But his stomach was talking. His little feet went one in front of the other, and his legs kept moving in search of ... what?

Night fell suddenly, and Thomas didn't have a chimney in sight. There would not be a convenient rock ledge to shelter him, either. But he couldn't change anything. He was cold and tired in body but not in spirit. He said his prayers out loud while he lay under a fallen log of huge proportion. "Thank ye, God fer gettin' me this fur. Sure would like some food ... kinda tired of drinkin' water from a stump. Keep me and Brooks and Toy an' everybody safe all night. Goodnight. Amen."

Thomas had crossed over many hills, ridges, and swollen creeks. There was determination in his soul. The next morning, the sun woke him and stirred his determination. He rose to his feet and immediately began a search for fresh water to start the day. It felt good not to have to fill two buckets of water, but it did not feel as good as the thought of "who" was drawing the water now that he was out of reach.

It still made sense to keep moving up and to search for smoke. The day progressed on, and the hunger pressed in. There was not a cabin in sight—not one. Thomas kept crossing over ridges and over swollen creeks with water rushing so fast that he was too intimidated to cross. He was forced to find better paths where it was more narrow and calm. He never learned to swim. Mama was frightened of the water and made her children keep their distance.

The hunger was painful, and Thomas had to search hard for water to drink. His plan was to find smoke from a cabin, so he slowed his climb and turned his focus to the valley below. He had to stop and rest. His body was ready to be still, and his side hurt from the straining. How far had he gotten? Was it going to be far enough?

He could hear the sound of water farther down the mountain. "I hope I find it afore dark." He forced himself to move. His head hurt, but he didn't know why. The blame would most likely be put on hunger; it was overwhelming him, and he hadn't the strength to fight it off. He searched for smoke or anything that might mean shelter from the coming darkness. A sudden feeling of being lost came over him. He picked up his pace and headed towards the sound of water and HOPE.

The stream was small but satisfying. He lie on his stomach, scooping up the water into his hand. Then he put his lips to the surface and drank for a long time. This boy felt the weight of being alone in the world. And the struggle began because of the fall of darkness upon everything around him. He had to find a place to hide—to hide from the unknown shadows. It would have to be a heap of leaves that had collected against the base of three oak trees. He stumbled because of weakness, but he landed well, cradled in a nest of sorts.

The moon and stars were out, and as Thomas lie on his back, he looked and listened. More leaves were popping out on the limbs of the trees, and the dogwoods were in blossom. The wind made sweet whispers that swept down the mountain and helped comfort the boy. But then the hoot-owl hooted and completely unsettled Thomas. His head and side were hurting, and all he really wanted was to rest. Again, the hoot-owl made its call.

A haunting memory was also making its call on Thomas. It was a dark night. He was holding Brook's hand and running through the woods. The scenes were alive with movement in Thomas's mind. Mama was in front of them. She was running, too, and looking over her shoulder with a frightened look and wrinkled brow. They were all running downhill, away from the cabin. "Keep quiet, we're goin' to sleep under the stars t'night. I got it all ready fer us. It'll be jest us." She was slowing down and looking back over her shoulder and over their heads. Just past the cedar thicket, she stopped. "Boys, hol' still 'til I get our fixin's." Mama pulled a wood box out from under a tree. "See, here's our beds," she spread out two quilts. Baby Toy wanted to crawl away. She caught him and made them all lie still, side-by-side.

Then she covered them all with another quilt. She sat in front of them, seated on the box. She was watching over them. The hoot-owl "who-whoed" its call. She sensed Thomas was frightened. "Look up at the stars winkin' at y'uns. Do y'uns know why the owl makes that sound? The daddy owl is sangin' to his sweetheart. It's a sweet song—a love song. The daddy owl and his lady owl love each other fer life. Their love runs so deep that they love and keer fer one another all their days. What yer hearin' is their "love talk".

"Mama, why is it always dark when they talk? Do they sleep all day, like father does?" Thomas asked.

"No, son. It h'aint like 'at. God made hit thataway. It t'weren't made to make us a'feared. Hit's encouragement from creation to us, to yuns. Don't be a'feared." She made everything sound so settled and acceptable.

Thomas tossed and turned all night, and the owl was not to blame. He was hungry, and his head and side hurt. At first light, he rose and stumbled to the creek for a drink. He stayed there a long time, resting his aching head on his arms. What was he to do next? "I don't know whar ta turn next." He felt like he was shouting. He looked down at his arms and saw dirt. His hands were filthy, and black dirt was under his fingernails. "I gotta git up and git goin'. No one's out lookin' fer me."

And up he got headed downhill. That was all he could make his legs and feet do.

Weakness caught up to him, and he fell to his knees. He couldn't help himself. He covered his pale blue eyes with his dirty little hands and wept. "Oh, Mama, Mama! Come git me. But no one hears me." With aching heart and tightly shut eyes, the reality hit his thoughts like a hard kick to the stomach. *Mama is dead. DEAD! That's how this whole nightmare started. This whole wicked, hateful thang began because Mama ...* There was no lie in his thoughts. The whole injustice was set into motion that first day without Mama.

The boy was drifting in and out of consciousness. There was a genuine sound of desperation to his sobs, and waves of pain were washing over him. Thomas's cries echoed across the mountain. Someone did hear, and someone was watching him. That someone was standing watch from behind a blossoming dogwood tree.

Thomas would not be able to recognize this man by his face, but it was the Indian Hunter who had saved him once before. Thomas was trying to focus on this man's movements, but he could not, for weakness had overtaken him. Quietly, the Indian Hunter moved towards Thomas's limp body and with great care, lifted him, and whispered, "It will be all right, my son. Rest."

The Indian Hunter did not rest, but instead, he quickened his pace in a definite direction. Haste was not mixed with jolting or shaking. The boy's condition could not take violence. Man and boy were as one, and the Hunter's maneuverings were much like that of the cat that he had killed. The only reason he stopped was to offer the boy a drink from his water skin and to wipe his brow.

Thomas was too sick to confidently recognize the Indian, and what few words did escape his feverish lips were gibberish. Instinctually, the Indian knew when it was time to rest. How tender were his attentions toward Thomas. The Indian, with Thomas in his strong arms again, set his quick feet on a distinct path. Down the mountain the path led, and in no time, they were crossing a narrow ridge.

The Indian's familiarity with the surroundings was astounding. He never stumbled or slipped in his footing, even carrying Thomas in the dark. He did not have to stop to get his bearings. His feet took them to the perfect resting spot beneath the ridge on a well-worn path that twisted and climbed between huge ferns and enormous trees stretching Heavenward. A creek of good size ran parallel to the path. Thomas was placed tenderly on a soft bed of leaves and ferns. The Indian removed a blue cloth covering from the knapsack that crossed his body. He lovingly covered Thomas. His stong hand lifted the little boy's head for another drink. Thomas was too sick, in both heart and body, to notice.

The winds of change were blowing down on that mountain. It was TIME. A TIME of fulfillment. Thomas had an appointment to keep. An appointed TIME of great importance. Would it be his TIME to join his Mama in Heaven, fulfilling her promise, finally? It would most certainly be the most obvious answer to all of the problems bearing down on him, presently. His thoughts moved with the hunger and pain in his body.

"I'll jest close my eyes," he whispered, "and when I wake, I'll be some whar nice. I won't be hungry and my head ..."

With Thomas securely in his arms again, the Indian continued down the steep embankment. Thomas felt like he was floating as if he had wings. To Thomas, everything felt like a dream—a wonderful dream. The voice of the creek "tinkled" in his ears, and the ferns sang a lullaby in chorus with the birds. The heartbeat of the Indian tapped against Thomas's cheek.

It said, "It … will be … all right … my son …" and the trees whispered, "Rest, rest … It … will be … all right … my son … Rest, rest."

Part 2
Thomas Alva

16

Appointments

John Barnett Mountain was all a buzz with accounts of storm damage. Livestock was missing, and winds had flattened entire barns. Fallen trees blocked wagon roads, and many creeks had overflowed their banks, making lakes of several of the farmers' fields.

But word had been sent to Bitsy to come quick. Damage or not, she must make her way, somehow. She packed her leather bag—twice. It was her habit of years and years of experience to check and recheck. "Mussn't leave nothin' out … never know what cha might need." She was needed, for another baby wanted to make its entrance into the world, and she knew they don't always come easy. Most things in this life don't come without a cost, especially the ones of value. Now that her bags were ready, the only thing needed was a little more light.

The Ragsdale family lived a ways back on Cripple Creek, at least a two hours climb up from the mill. Bitsy's husband, Wick, had reminded her to stick to the known path. "Darlin', if'n ya need he'p, thar would be at least one cabin ta shelter ya, if need be. I'll be right c'here, waitin' fer ya." She knew her way to Cripple Creek, and Wick was silly to be worried. The sun was peeking around corners with encouragement. With her bag slung across her shoulder and her hand on her hip, she waited for Wick to bend over and kiss her on the forehead.

She returned this kiss with one to Wick's cheek, and then she hurried her short little legs. She had to get to this woman. It was a first baby. *Sometimes them first 'uns is the worriest 'uns*, she thought to herself. But she whistled out loud, through her teeth.

Bitsy's real name was Betsy Evangeline Davis Miller, a name way too big for such a petite lady. She stood four feet, 11 inches tall. It was her generosity that made her famous across that mountain. For she knew when someone was in real need, and she gave where she could. From a young age, she stood up for the oppressed and looked to the needs of the poor. More cabins than not were at one time or another recipients of her gifts of food and clothing. She earned the mountain folks' respect and love, for she cherished her relationships. Once while she was out to pick berries for a pie, she happened upon a woman who had been cornered by a young bear. Bitsy distracted that bear and frightened him away.

Because of her boldness and caring, it was natural for Bitsy to learn the discipline of midwifery. She and Rosey Hodges were the only trained and trustworthy midwives in those hills.

Today was another one of those days when she was needed. Birthing was serious business. She treated it as a gift from above. A gift of great responsibility. Bitsy couldn't imagine life any different.

But there had been a time when they had hoped for more.

How deep the little woman's thoughts were as she climbed the path. She all but ignored the steep section of the climb—with the birds chirping and the new life budding all around her. *What a diff'rence a day makes. Here's hopin' "joy" comes in the mornin', or should I say "jack"? Might be Ragsdale babies come quick. But not a fore I git thar. God he'p us all, but I gotta herry.*

But it would be impossible to "herry." The storm had claimed the life of Founder's Tree, and it lay smack across the one and only passage to Squirrel Hollow on Cripple Creek. The huge tree was ancient, but the deluge of the two-day storm kept its roots from holding their claim to life and the lovely landscape had been erased.

"Well, I'll be jiggered," Bitsy said as she rode up to the tree. "What's a gal ta do? They's no ladder in my bag ... so goin' over hit is out of the question." The creek had definitely overflowed its banks with vengeance, and the proof was the new steep drop to the creek. It was decidedly more danger than she wanted to entertain.

The mission in front of her caused Bitsy to walk away from the edge and move closer to the mountainside. "I've got ta be wise 'bout this tricky path. Thar's no roots to grab holt of ta git ta higher ground," she said as she looked behind her at the wall of mud and tangled roots. "But maybe I can squeeze through this crack under he'a." Some light was seeping out from a small space between the fallen tree and the now muddy bank that had once been its residence. She bent over and removed some of the debris from the crack. "O, Lord make me slick as grease and as thin as a corn fritter." She pushed her leather bag through first, letting it land wherever. Then she sucked in her stomach, pressed her back against the earthen wall, and proceeded to inch her way through the crack.

It took almost no effort at all, which completely surprised her and caused an embarrassing remark to escape her lips—some remembered words about not borrowing trouble for tomorrow. But trouble was not what greeted her on the other side.

As she bent over to retrieve her bag, something flew across her face and forced her to lose her balance. Down she went, hard, right on her behind. Curiosity got the best of her. "Was that a blue bird? I coulda swore I saw somethin' blue ... She turned her head to the left, gasped, and exclaimed, "Mercy sakes alive!"

A mountainous pile of debris had rolled down the narrow road completely making passage impossible. But that was not all. The debris sheltered something covered with a blue piece of cloth—indigo blue, the kind of blue rarely seen in those hills. Bitsy made her way forward, still on hands and knees. She was not quite sure what was causing the feeling of urgency, but it drove her forward. Gently she extended her arm through the tangled roots and limbs. "God, he'p me. He'p me, please." She was holding her breath as she lifted the cloth. "A chile, a chile," the discovery came in whispers. She placed her skilled hand on its brow. "H'its burnin' up with fever."

She gathered up her skirts, slung her bag across her, squeezed back through to the other side of the tree, and ran for home. "O, Lord make me swift as downhill waters. That chile depends on it! O, God git Wick ready to he'p ... What is it we're to do?" It was miraculous how quickly she arrived at the mill.

"Wick! Wick! Come quick!," she called with desperate voice. "Whar ere ya! He's gonna die, he's gonna die." From the corner of the rock wall, Wick came on the run. "Darlin' I'm here … now what in blue blazes …" he reached her and grabbed her shoulders to steady her.

"On the path, on the path at Founder's Tree. Get the wagon." She was crying and trying to talk at the same time. "A chile, a boy chile. Go git him, Wick. He's dyin'! Git him to Rosie. She'll know whar to find Doc. She'll be down to the post office. Look fer a blue keever in the brush … way behind the tree." She was sprinting towards the barn and still crying but mostly shouting. "Ya better herry, h'it ain't too late—yet. I knowed it in my innerds. I'm gonna ride Myrtle t'other side of the crick. Then cut back across. Don't yun's werry 'bout me," she was already on Myrtle's bare back and kicking her sides.

Wick had been loading bags of corn meal into the wagon for his monthly delivery to town and so horse and wagon were ready. Wick, with running steps jumped up to the seat and snapped the reins. He headed up the path at a gallop's pace. Under his breath, Wick repeated Bitsy's descriptions. "A boy chile, under a blue, a blue keever … Founder's Tree." This was no nightmare, no trick. The severity of this situation was written all over Bitsy's face.

The terrain had definitely changed with the storm, making the already narrow path precarious to navigate. His next greatest need was a place to turn the wagon around so that it would be less complicated to have the rig ready for its swift flight down the hillside in search of Rosie and Doc. His eyes were looking up in search of Founder's Tree. He couldn't see it, yet. "I'll turn 'er 'round here. Timmy, you'll wait fer me. Whoa, boy." He could trust that horse to be right there when he got back.

"What has happen' to the tree?" And then, he got his answer. It lay across the little road. "Look fer the chile, look fer the blue …" and there it was in front of the fallen landmark. Wick ran the rest of the way.

"Oh, no! What's a man to do?" With careful fingers, he touched the light curls that stuck out from under the blue coverlet. He turned back the blue fabric almost whispering his question to the boy, "What's yer name, chile?" There was no answer, and it was a heavy breathing noise which made Wick almost snatch him up. The boy's fever penetrated every piece of fabric between them, including the blue coverlet. Wick was convinced to hasten his stride. Bitsy had read things rightly. A battle for life or death was being fought—right in front of him. Right in his arms.

The boy weakly moaned and groaned when Wick lay him on the bags. He placed him close within his reach—not that there was one single thing he could do for him. He could do nothing but fly like the wind down that path and hope that he knew where to find Rosie and the Doc.

Everything was crowded together in Wick's brain. How was he to know what to do next? What if he couldn't find Doc or Rosie? He comforted himself as he said, "One werry at the time, Wick ol' man. Jest git down this mess of a road." He was encouraged when the boy made sounds; the sounds were what was urging man and horse to risk their lives.

It was a long, steep journey to town. It took more than an hour, more closely to two hours from the mill to the post office. Wick was sweating and his knuckles were white from managing Timmy and the wagon. It wouldn't do to throw either one out of the wagon. "Look for Rosie! Look for Rosie!" He was repeating his beloved's instructions again. A growing feeling of desperation made him begin to shout long before the building was even in sight. Driven by responsibility and fear, Wick stood up, shouting her name. "Rosie! Rosie Hodges!" Wick's neck was straining to help make his voice heard. Closer to the post office, he yelled, "Fer God's sake, Rosie, HE'P!"

There was no answer. "Maybe I jest didn't hear fer the racket I was makin'." He was slowing down the rig then from a seated position. He wasn't going to give up, yet. He checked on the boy again. *Why was everythin' so quiet, today? Whar are all tha people?*

"Rosie, Rosie, ROSIE!" he yelled. He frantically searched with his eyes from one side of the dirt road to the other. There was not even one child in sight. "Rosie Hodges, can ye hear me? HE'P! Bitsy said ya was here! I need the Doc! I need him—NOW!" His voice screeched like a war cry and then made pitiful calls that hung in the air as if he were a desperate little boy calling for his Mama.

"Wickham Miller, what is yer problem! Hur' I am! Behind ye." Wick stopped the horse, almost causing Timmy to sit down—he had pulled so hard. He jumped down, running the distance to Rosie Hodges. Rosie's arms were full, and a parcel poked out of the top of her doctoring bag. Before either of them could speak a word, the boy on the sacks began to weakly cry aloud. "Mama, Mama is it safe ta come out?" He was flailing his arm in a weak sort of motion. Rosie and Wick simultaneously jumped into the back of the wagon. She emptied her arms and grasped to gain control the boy's arms. "Chile, I'm here. H'it's all right, now." The boy relaxed into unconsciousness. Wick planted himself on the wagon bench and ordered Timmy to "Giddy up, boy!"

Rosie Hodges was the best midwife and physician's assistant known. Wick knew this, knew it as well as he knew his own name, but he was scared and worried just the same. She was cradling the boy's entire body in her arms and lap while speaking gently and quietly and as her hands skillfully moved to understand this body.

"Wick, Doc is somewhar down south a town. I ain't sure whar, though. Holler, holler loud!" and they both did just that. There wasn't another house in sight. John Barnett Mountain was a settlement, and its people had scattered themselves all over those hills. They only came to the post office to trade and send a letter if they hadn't seen the post rider in too long a time. Wick turned eastward, towards his in-laws' homestead.

"Stop the wagon, I gotta check on thangs. Oh my, he ain't got any meat on his bones, Wick. Skin and bones, t'ain't hardly any color to his flesh. Whar d'ye find 'im?" Rosie was lifting up the eyelids to look into the boy's eyes and peering into his mouth.

"I fount him right whar Bitsy tol' me ta look. At Founder's Tree, only t'weren't 'xac'ly thar ..."

A cheery "ha-looo" wafted down the hill. "I heered ye hollerin'!"

It was Doc! Joseph Williams was a native of that mountain, and he knew every piece of gossip and truth those hills had to divulge. This time, however, he had no way of knowing what was happening just then—until he heard Wick's hollerin'. He jumped into the wagon, knelt over the child in Rosie's lap, and no one made a sound. He was already opening his bag. Instinct and experience were the driving forces.

The two adults in the wagon needed no verbal communication. Their history of working together for so many years made everything they did look like a beautiful dance. Wick watched and wiped the drops of sweat still streaming from his brow. He couldn't help, but he had to hope they could do something for this child. Wick's thoughts tormented him, *H'it might be too late. Oh, don't let it be, don't let his little life be taken. Not yet!* Almost out loud he was reasoning, "I was too skeert ta go any faster, h'it might a done him more harm." He was waiting … and wringing his hands.

"Wick, git us to Mournin' Dove Chapel. That's as fur as we dare ta go. He won't make it t' no train depot. Don't spare the horse … and pray!"

17

Open Doors

For the four people travelling in the wagon, TIME was not a friend. No, this was a crisis. All manner of skill and wisdom was being summoned. Doc and Rosie were focused on the boy child. Wick was focused on the two big hairpin curves that had to be managed in just the right way. He could take no chances with this precious cargo. The good news was that Wick and Timmy were old hats with this part of the road. They had been down this road in both daylight and darkness when Wick was courting Bitsy. Those were happy times—so full of love and hope for the future. Right then, though, time was being marked by a fast horse and a steady driver.

Thankfully the previous storm had not taken the bridge out and crossing was over in a wink. Doc got out over the side of the wagon and helped Rosie off the end of it. He and Rosie had already moved the boy close to the end to help transport him. Now came Doc's instructions for Wick. "Keerful, when I call fer ye, bring him into the chapel. We got to get thangs ready. No need to worry." Doc and Wick already had an understanding. Together, they had fought DEATH. Everything was said that needed to be said with one simple look from one man into the other man's eyes.

The simple wooden door of Mournin' Dove Chapel was pushed open, then quickly closed. It remained so for what seemed like hours. But Wick knew the boy didn't have hours. The child had been swaddled in his blue blanket by Rosie and left for him to watch over. Wick stood there helpless and anxious. Doc's eyes were his reassurance that the right thing was going to be done. But there was a wrestling in Wick's soul. The outcome of all things was in the hands of someone else …

Rosie stood in the doorway, calling to him with a whistle. It was with great tenderness and with long strides that the child was brought into the chapel. Wick adjusted his eyes to the lighting in the space. Doc gently instructed, "Lay him down, and then I want cha to find all the lamps and candles ye can. I'll talk to ye when ye git back." Doctor and assistant moved together in one motion, removing the blue blanket then the boy's clothing. Wick went on his search.

When he returned, Wick found that a table had been set up near the boy's head. Small glass bottles and metal trays, along with neatly arranged instruments, had carefully been laid out. He stared at the scene in silence, but his whole being was registering the seriousness of the situation. Only the little body that lay moaning and pale looked out of place. Doc took the lamps from his hands and placed them on a smaller table.

"Don't go anywhar, Wick. Stay outside. Won't need ye in here. No matter what, don't let anyone, DO YA HEAR ME? Don't let anyone in here."

Wick's eyes were locked onto Doc's eyes, and even though the words were barely spoken above a whisper, they had been plenty powerful. The doctor returned to his patient. Wick turned himself about, and as silently as he could manage, he exited the chapel and held the knob until it softly latched.

His feet took him to the wagon, and habit moved his hands to find the feedbag for Timmy. But he could not think of food or of anything—his heart was fixed on the unknown.

18

Who Knew?

Myrtle and Bitsy found the old Indian trail dry and easy to read. The journey would have been the perfect opportunity for Bitsy to relax and consider the expectant family's different personalities. Usually she recited her "talk" to the new dad, adding what would appropriately apply. Her mind would have been fixed on saving her strength so that the new mom could rely on her when her own strength was failing. She normally would have given in to all of her habits of preparation ... but her mind was screaming!

Who's chile was he? How'd he get there? Did Wick get there in time? Oh, Lord, let it not be too late, let it not be too late. I've seen with my own two eyes how ye take keer of life. I ain't sure what ta say but he'p. The fact that she had left a helpless child alone in the woods even to go for help tortured her. Leaving to bring a firstborn child into this world should have been a comfort, but how could she ever forget that little face full of fever and pain?

Myrtle was enjoying her spring journey and paid no mind to Bitsy's sniffling and mumbling. All on her own, Myrtle picked up her hooves, plodded forward and upward to climb the hills, and finally crossed Cripple Creek without getting Bitsy flustered or wet. Bitsy swung her leg over the horse and slid down to the ground. It would be impossible to get to the Ragsdale's on the back of an animal. So with her skirts gathered in one hand, her birthing bag across her shoulder, and Myrtle's reins in the other, Bitsy made her way on foot to Squirrel Hollow. Someone was waiting for her—waiting for her gentle, kind, dependable presence.

Red Ragsdale greeted Bitsy as she walked up. "Well, lookey who's fin'ly made it."

Then he turned his head to call his wife: "Hey, hon! The midwife's hur, ye can stop yer frettin'! Boy, howdy! I sure am glad ye made it. I ain't so sure I woulda done much good." Red then led good old Myrtle to the lean-to in order to be fed and watered, and when Red looked back toward Bitsy, she could see the relief written all over his young face.

She was needed now. It was nice to be needed. It produced a feeling of purpose, and the feeling would have to suffice. Bitsy's mind let go of the boy under the blue coverlet as she removed her bag. She was remembering what had started this day. TIME was marching on while she completely filled the atmosphere of the small cabin she was entering. "Well, how is the little Mama? Let's git our hands warshed and our sleeves rolled up ... a messenger came with news somebody wants a birthday ... and we'll need some light."

Red was going to need to stay out of their way, so Bitsy created lots of busy work for him, including several trips to the creek and more firewood for the fire they "might need." Red and Liza Jane were young and much in love. When Red was 19, he had asked for Liza Jane's hand in marriage. She was 15 then—sort of old by mountain standards. It was Liza Jane's Paw that made them wait until Red had his homestead and cash money saved up. But nevertheless, they were perfect for each other, and the wait was of no consequence. The real problem came because everyone waits where babies are concerned. Red Ragsdale was terrible, downright miserable, to deal with because of all this waiting.

Liza Jane was a wonder! She was showing Bitsy all the darling little clothes she had made for the coming child. Red had traded for an old-fashioned baby cradle, which was proudly displayed by the hearth. Truly, Liza Jane's pride and joy was the little quilt she had made for "him." She was convinced it was going to be a boy, and was just about to tell Bitsy the name when the real contractions seized her.

How many times had Bitsy seen that look on a woman's face? That look when she realizes that there is NO GOING BACK! The life inside her has determined it wants OUT! It almost made her chuckle. She mused, "They all get that same look a shock on their face." Bitsy knew better than to laugh just then. "What name did ye say?" She was up to her old tricks. Busy work.

Bitsy could now rest on the hearth bench that she had pulled up close to the bed. Liza Jane's contractions never let up, and just before the rooster crowed, Zachary Michael Ragsdale made his entrance into that cabin. Red and Liza Jane had worked together during the dark hours of her labor. Bitsy was proud—quite proud—of the two of them. It seemed to her that the busy work produced two levelheaded adults, which made her job all the easier.

Mother and baby were doing just what they needed to do— sleeping. And Red was sleeping, too, curled up at the foot of the bed. Just what the doctor ordered! A perfect picture of love to go with Bitsy's much needed cup of coffee. It was perfect, right there in the Ragsdale's cabin. She took another sip, confirming what she felt right then: "All is right, and God is in His Heaven ... and with Doc and Rosie and the chile. I'll have to be patient. Cain't rush off an' abandon my post. Besides, what could I do diff'rnt. I kin pray here jest as good as anywhar."

19

Babies, None

Man and horse had spent the night out-of-doors, waiting near Mournin' Dove Chapel. The man pacing. The horse resting, tied to a Hickory tree in the cemetery. Hours and hours of fretting for the man—without his pipe and tobacco. He could not smoke his pipe as it had been left back at the house. Smoking always helped him to think. He wished for something else to do, besides think. While standing amongst the grave markers, he shivered—but not because of the cool night air.

Ghostly voices and old conversations were jumping out at Wick. They were plotting against him. HOPELESSNESS and DEATH wanted him to remember what had happened. This was their chance to win—to finally make him give in. He was choking back the tears that the voices were dragging forward. The last encounter had happened so long ago, but in the darkness and with all that was happening inside the chapel just now, he wasn't strong enough to hold them back. Why was it never pleasant when Doc and he had to be together? When Bitsy was the patient and Wick was the one who had to wait, Doc Williams had been the one with all the strength.

That old scene played again in his mind. "Wick, now, we've all done all we could. I was hopin' I'd never have to say these words ... The baby ... yur son is dead .... wait ... thar's more. H'it's Betsy. Rosie's with her but...she's had it rough. An' h'it was diffrnt from the last baby. I cain't explain it jest now, she needs me. An' she'll need you worse ..."

Why, oh why did he have to remember the losses? He thought those memories and conversations were buried there in that cemetary. Wick was unable to keep his composure in the face of those grave markers. His hands now covered his tear-soaked face. Wick's old grief forced a new prayer from his lips.

"God, I swore at ye and said I'd never forgive ye. I vowed to myse'f I'd never trust ye, with nothin'. I've run from ye, hard, and all the while, shuttin' Betsy out … a cuttin' off her hopes and dreams. Ever time her heart was beggin' ye for a chile an' t'weren't no real hope thar, h'it was you I blamed. She kept lovin' and trustin' ye, and I jest couldn't watch the pain in her face no more.

"They's three of our babies here under this very ground. Ten years of her believin' and me a hatin' and actin' a fool. Cain't no one change what's in the past. We wanted them babies, we wanted to love 'em and keer fer 'em.

I ain't so bad, am I? Can ye forgive me, please God? I kin see how h'it matters to ye, the lovin' and the hopin'. Pleeeze, God." He was crumpling to the ground under the weight of this old struggle. As the hot, salty tears dropped down, the grown man gave himself over to the child within as waves of sorrow, grief, and remorse brought a change of heart. With that old fight finally over, Wick could surrender to a peaceful, much needed rest. A merciful slumber blanketed Wick right there amoungst the graves.

It was the sure sound of wagon wheels that disturbed Wick's sleep. Someone was heading towards the bridge. "What day is this? Is it Sunday? It is Sunday." Wick knew now who was in that wagon, heading for Mournin' Dove Chapel. Brother Bill Downs was making his way to the chapel to tidy things up and light the lamps and candles.

But Doc and Rosie and the child must not be disturbed. Wick had been entrusted with that responsibility. Sunday or not—no one was going to make a sound or go near that door. No sounds had been coming from the building, and Wick had not seen hide nor hair of either Doc or Rosie since he had closed the door at sunset. So, Wick set out to stop that wagon and Brother Bill before they got to the chapel.

"Brother Bill, I know yer not 'spectin' to see me hur but they's somethin' ye need ta know. And they's somethin' we gotta do, together." Wick, as briefly as he could, told the story of the boy and how Doc and Rosie had spent the previous night operating on the child. Brother Bill could not have been any more surprised than if a real lightning bolt had struck him.

"Brother Bill, we have to keep folks from turnin' into the chapel today. Sarvices'll have ta be canceled." The two men blocked the wagon path with their rigs and waited at the road's edge.

It was Brother Bill who decided to send everyone to his house for a prayer gathering instead. "T'aint no use jawin' hur in tha yard when prayin's what's needed," And with that announcement, he headed home.

Within an hour that local Sunday-go-to-meetin' crowd was all gathered at the Downs' place. It was an hour later that Rosie came out and whistled for Wick.

The walk to the chapel door was way too long for Wick. He had hoped to be able to read Rosie's face and get the news. It was Doc who met him and straight away laid out the facts.

With one hand on Wick's shoulder and the other rubbing his own forehead, Doc began his tale of what he and Rosie had experienced. "He was full of pizen, from his appendix. It was a mess to figure out. That boy … that boy has had it rough afore he got truly sick. Most likely, he's older than he looks an' somebody has used … But I'm rabbit trailin' … Wick we cain't move him jest now. As fur as doctorin' goes, t'aint nothin' else ta do fer him. He don't need nothin' 'cept rest and peace. I aim to give 'im that. I know ye'd had a rough go of it, keepin' watch outside but now ye can keep watch whilst we rest." He slipped around the corner of the table and took Rosie's place beside the boy and watched him breathe.

The chapel remained undisturbed until the sun was setting. Gentleness and quiet blanketed the inside of the chapel. The most gentle of noises broke the silence. It was the welcome tap of Sister Downs signaling that food had arrived. Brother Bill stayed just long enough to get the report and to leave two quilts and two feather pillows for the weary heads that saved a child's life. Gifts from the prayer gathering.

The blue coverlet lay neatly folded under the little boy's head. The little face looked calm and peaceful—not at all recognizable when compared to the face Wick had first touched. He could tell Rosie had washed the boy for there was no more mud across his forehead, and the leaves and moss had been removed from his right ear. While the boy was breathing, the big shouldered, strong-armed man in dirty overalls lay his work-worn hand as close to touching him as he dared.

TIME came and went, passing through that chapel of peace. LIFE had wandered in, and decided to stay because of the HOPE and ENCOURAGEMENT from all the adults who had come to the rescue of this boy.

Doc's promise of letting the boy rest under a peaceful roof was realized. Not one soul standing guard or resting would have allowed any interruption. Too much neglect had been tolerated in regards to the little frame lying on the table.

And as he lay, comforted initially by the hands that operated on him, he slept without the knowledge that an entire mountain now knew of him. Neither his origin or his real intended destination mattered. Nor did they weigh themselves down with such pointless issues. The people of John Barnett Mountain had instead bent their knees to petition Heaven to stay the hand of DEATH.

They would one day give a witness of thanks to the brave ones who heard the cries of this helpless, sick boy. TIME would give every last one of them answers … in its own good time, of course.

20

Questions but No Answers

Liza Jane and Zachary were getting well acquainted. Bitsy and Red kept things running smoothly. It had always been Bitsy's main focus, after getting her patients delivered, to make sure the new mom produced plenty of milk. That took real patience, sometimes.

Nobody but Red needed to get re-acquainted with the washboard and the clothes line. Bitsy knew this was not busy work designed to keep him distracted, but Red could not be convinced. She gathered her muster and re-stated how important it was for the new mom to remain calm and rested. After all, the new mom was the one on whom all the responsibilities landed, for everybody's sake. So, Bitsy stayed an extra day to reassure them all that life was going to be just fine.

Myrtle was more than ready to go back to her stall in the barn at home. Red had taken great care of her, but just the same, it was time to go home. Bitsy said and kissed all the good-byes that were called for, and she eagerly led Myrtle down the trail out of Squirrel Hollow. The greening of the earth was evident at every turn, and it made Bitsy want to hurry. The path made the decisions for the two of them though; it was definitely way too steep to do any sort of hurrying.

Bitsy's bag had nothing in it to snack on. She had prepared breakfast early in the day, and it was a toss-up as to which Ragsdale had the biggest appetite. She worked out a plan for Red to keep up with appetites and washing and NAPS! They were more important than the wash pile. Bitsy had also made an extra pan of biscuits and fried up more than enough ham. She even managed to make some ginger snap cookies. But she hid those from Red, and of course, she had told Liza Jane exactly where to find them.

"Now, missy, let's have a understandin' … day after t'morry ye can get up and maybe do some sweepin' and some dish warshin' but that's all … then ye can share them ginger snaps with Red … if'n he's done what I wrote on the list." All of this was made final by the wink of her right eye as she left the cabin.

Bitsy was free from her duty, and she could let her thoughts loose again. The scenes at Founder's Tree had been replaying in her mind. "Had to be a pesky blue bird a tryin' ta get my 'ttention! I hain't never seed the like!" As she remembered the episode, it was confirmed to her that she should not just think of the events as strange. Oh, everything about that day was decidedly strange, but it would be inaccurate to say strange was the only description. Strange indeed, and most likely miraculous—the tree, the hole left for her to squeeze through, the mysterious blue bird, the blue coverlet. She could only manage to say outloud, "My, my, my …"

After Liza Jane had spread her baby's quilt out for Bitsy to see, Bitsy had touched that cotton fabric and been reminded of that blue coverlet. There hadn't been a proper time to think upon all of that until now, and she liked everything thought-through and properly labeled. "Of all the purdy thangs I've ever see'd … there h'aint been nothin' to beat that blue keever. Who could a made such a thang? … I shore don't know no body." An instant lump of emotion choked her, and her eyes filled with involuntary tears.

She more than hoped everything was all right. Every time she had held the new baby, she had thoughts of the sick child and of Wick. And then the questions would begin to roll around in her head … without answers. It was to her Heavenly Father that she had taken the questions and requests for intervention on behalf of the boy. But she was left knowing full well that the answers would not be the immediate kind.

The journey home was as quick as a mountain journey could be. A slow, but deliberate duo moved along as fast as they dared. Bitsy was more tired than she thought, and she was thankful that the mule was there to carry her home. Myrtle was dependable, like herself. Like Wick. Like Doc and Rosie. The boy could depend on them all. She not only hoped that he was alive but also she hoped that he felt no ill will toward her for having left him there under the debris. Surely he understood.

Her own head was hurting smartly as testimony to all of her worrying. Add to that, she had been physically drained at the Ragsdale's, and she could not wait to get home. She had had to sleep in interrupted shifts and on a makeshift bed. She had run out of clean clothes, the outside kind and the inside kind. And she had needed to bathe and to scrub. One look at her and Wick would necessarily insist that she bathe and go to bed. She would not have to be convinced, and she was too weary to argue.

As she closed in on home, several light sources illuminated the whole area. The sun had already set, and the usual quiet mill looked wide awake and ready for something. Bitsy's custom was to holler for Wick as she neared the house, but she didn't have the strength. He was usually watching for her, anyway. But Wick was not there. He was not anywhere. Instead it was Brother Bill that met her on the trail ready to help. She wanted to ask questions, but the pain in her head didn't let any words out. He silently led the way to the barn. At the barn, four more men were there to help Bitsy dismount and to help carry her things. Brother Bill took her arm and walked with her to the house. Once they were out of earshot of the men, he spoke. "Bitsy, Sweetie, Oh, thar's so much to tell ye, an' I want to tell it all … but you look plumb wore out. Don't fret 'bout nothin'. The boy is still awful sick and Doc won't let anyone near 'im—plumb ordered us all to stay away and to keep peace. Wick ain't hur, yet. It'll be nearer noon t'morry. Brother Bill has it all taken keer of. Yer old friend Nellie Weathers is goin' to wait on ye hand an' foot.

I want cha ta go in an' git yer bathin' and dressin' over. Nellie'll let me know when yer settled in bed an' I'll come talk to ye then." Brother Bill had always been truthful and father-like to her. All her life, he had a way with her, a real relationship, which could make all her ruffled feathers smooth right out.

Nellie Weathers was her dearest friend, and one who always appeared when Bitsty needed comforting the most. But the two women who normally would have clucked like two young hens were quiet and gentle in their greeting. Bitsy undressed and stepped into the ready bathing tub. She halfway scrubbed herself, stood, and then rinsed the suds away with the warm pitcher of water. Her clean, warm underclothes and nightgown were quickly found on the back of her rocking chair beside the fire. Nellie was the one to credit with that sensible placement.

Bitsy slipped between her bed covers, which had been neatly folded back for her, and instinctually, Nellie brought a tray of goodies. Right behind her came Brother Bill entering the room almost silently. Bitsy sipped her chamomile tea, ignoring her fried eggs and fried apples, while Brother Bill told the story of the events that had taken place at Mournin' Dove Chapel.

It was a relief to finally know that the boy had made it through his surgery. That weight was finally lifting from Bitsy's shoulders. All of the players in this band had performed well—not missing a beat. It was just going to have to be that she was not going to have all her questions answered. The most important question had been answered by her Heavenly Father—it had not been too late for the boy-child! Bitsy bowed her head in silence, acknowledging her gratefulness to Him. TIME would have to permit the release of the answers to the rest of the questions.

Brother Bill came to a stopping point with a question for her. "Bitsy, where was it that ye came upon the chile? H'it sure would he'p if I knew some a yer story." She told him of the discovery of the fallen Founder's Tree and how she had to slip through the space to the other side. Next came the relation of the mysterious, persistant blue bird that contributed to her tumble causing the discovery of the blue coverlet that hid the boy. She could not refrain from telling of her journey back to the mill and owning up to her panic and desperation. And her tears were again proof of the pain it had caused her to leave the sick child.

"Sweetie, them fellers sleepin' in yer barn have been hur three days a workin' on Founder's Tree. I been out thar m'se'f and thar ain't no ways, no ways under Heaven that you could a squoze through … thar t'weren't no hole. The entire road was completely blocked off behine that tree. Why, hit was jammed by ever tree, twig, fern an' bush what got warshed downhill by the storm. They've sent fer he'p to bust through from t'other side so they kin git that tree cut up." Despite what his eyes had told him, Brother Bill had listened to Bitsy relay the story, he knew she wouldn't make up something like this. She had revealed everything that she remembered. He rubbed his chin, considering the possibility of another miracle.

21

Sisters

Before the dawn of the fourth day after the boy's surgery, Rosie had been sent away to deliver another baby. Doc Williams' patient was not completely out of danger, so Wick became the assistant. Many precautions had been taken to keep the chapel more like a hospital than a Sunday-go-to-meeting place. Wick's main responsibility was to keep things quiet and to help the doctor administer pain medication. The doctor was addressing the boy's needs as they arose, and with great concern, he asked Wick a difficult question.

"Have ye thought a what we're gonna do with him, next? He's hardly said three words together since his fever broke an' none of 'em give me no clues as to whar to send fer his fam'ly. I kin tell ye, as sure as shootin', I ain't so sure I want 'em ta come fetch him seein' how they's evidence they seem to plumb forgot ta feed 'im. An' thar's another thang ta be sure, unless he took a mighty big tumble all the way down a ravine, they's way too many bruises an' old scars fer my cumfert." They had both walked to the back of the room to discuss matters.

Wick had more than a dozen times realized that something was going to be needed next, he just wasn't sure what part he was to play. His head said send the boy to the Kentucky State Boy's Home in Lexington. But he knew the boy's life would have little value there, and besides, it was always overflowing. Once or twice, when there was work at the mill for two men, he considered going up there to get a helper.

But it was the hope and belief that Bitsy felt and voiced often, that yearning of being able to give Wick a child, that always stopped him dead in his thoughts.

Bitsy was nowhere near that chapel, and no one could be spared to fetch her. For all he knew, another baby had made its demands on her before she could get home. Brother Bill and the men had long since left to clean up the mess at Founder's Pass. So, there he was with only Doc to consult about the future.

"How long afore he'll be ready to move? He ain't awake long enough to even sit! An' all he's had to eat is broth and Sister Down's herb tea. I h'ain't seed what color eyes he's got. I h'ain't heard him speak, much less tell us his name."

"He don't need ta tell us nothin' right now. Wick, don't ye werry 'bout his appetite. Two days from now, he'll be talkin' and wantin' to run around. Ye still didn't answer my question, Wick. I'm convinced that hit'll take doct'rin' of a different sort ta heal this boy. He needs keerin' fer so his mind and his spirit kin he'p him heal. He's still in shock, I think, from the pizen an' the surgery … We'll werry 'bout this t'morry …" He turned back to his patient.

Wick turned his thoughts back to Bitsy. Back to the look of worry on her face when she sent him to fetch the child. He would never forget her sobs of desperation. That day was cemented in his memory, along with the change this boy had brought in his own heart. He wondered, *Without the night in the cemetery worryin' bout the little life inside the chapel, would he have made peace with God?* He had put all of those bitter reminders behind him. The right thing to do, for this boy and for Bitsy, would be to let her do what she was gifted to do … help bring life into the world.

With all of that Sovereign light shining down, the decision was therefore easily made. Wick himself found comfort in attending the little boy. His eyes were still not opened. So much mystery. How would Bitsy behave when the child came to their home? This boy child found in the debris of a storm was not the baby she had hoped for that was for certain. Whose child was he? Where were the parents? Too many questions—and no way to get answers just yet.

So when the evening meal was brought to the chapel, there was more to chew on than venison and potatoes. Sister Downs had come with her basket, and as usual, she was alone. "Doc, I'm sure thar's a rain a comin'. Most likely a hard two-day soakin'. I sure would rest easier if'in yuns would get the boy to more friendly quarters. Brother Downs left and took a team of men to clean up the mess at Founder's Pass. And I sent Nellie with Brother Downs to make things ready, that is in case yuns made up yer minds 'bout movin' him." Mable Downs was a gentle spirited woman; so, when she spoke, everyone listened—even the doctor.

"Well, Mable Downs! Ye jest read my mind! I was 'bout to tell Doc—we—Bitsy and me—would take keer of him until we all figured out whar he come from."

It was settled then and there, and then Sister Downs took over the "how to accomplish it" part. Everything was to begin at five o'clock in the morning, and there would be plenty of help. She had already thought everything through, and the two men were glad.

Even though the settlers of John Barnett Mountain were poor—Appalachian Mountain poor—there were beautiful signs of generosity. And since most were not afraid of hard work, the early morning assignment was greeted with excitement and with wonder. They knew how hard life was, and naturally they wanted to give whatever they could that would make this journey a little more comfortable. No one knew yet what was going to happen to this child, nor did they know whether or not he would live through the ordeal. For now, the boy held on to LIFE, and they were excited to be an encouraging force.

LIFE—it seemed—had been standing still. The whole mountain had held its breath and prayed for what felt like a long time. It was as if the whole world had stopped to permit the doctor to focus on the little child—and it seemed as if TIME had been standing still just for him.

Timmy was now standing still in front of the chapel doors. He was hitched to the wagon, which was full. Fresh hay and a feather bed awaited the boy. All kinds of food were piled under the wagon bench, some wrapped in cloth, some in brown paper, and some in precious glass canning jars.

Sister Downs held the door open while Doc and two women

waited for the boy to be transferred from Wick's arms to the traveling bed. The darkness was broken with multiple lanterns and HOPE. This dark was exciting.

HOPE had entered the scene and sat down right next to Wick on the bench.

Clean, fresh, beautiful quilts were lovingly placed on and around the little frame of a child, along with words, whispered prayers, and sweet songs of encouragement.

"Walk on, Timmy. We're goin' home." Timmy knew what that meant. But the voice sounded new and hopeful, instead of weighted down and tired and short-tempered. Wick was a new man. But he wondered: *Would the boy be new again, or was the infection too much?* TIME would tell. Doc still looked worried.

The mountain folk, standing shoulder to shoulder, waved goodbye and marked the event with unified silence. Praying.

22

Too Much Spring

On her way home, Bitsy saw the tree. A pink dogwood. No matter what direction the trail turned her, it was in her face. It stood out like an accidental brush stroke on a clean canvas. Arrow wood is the native name of the tree, for it is the Indians' favored wood to make arrows with because of its strength. But mountain folklore tells of the tree's other strong reminder—the shedding of innocent blood. According to an Indian legend, an Indian princess was murdered by the brave she rejected. Her blood mingled with the dogwood blossoms that lay with her on the ground. Eventually the tips of the blossoms turned pink.

Bitsy was a little girl when Brother Bill had told her that story. At that time, he had also told her his belief that the dogwood tree was blushing with embarrassment because it was the very tree used for Christ's crucifixion. The tree was frightfully and altogether beautiful as it was stirring up painful memories. The trail moved onward toward the mill. Toward home. Toward the unknown and the familiar.

All night Bitsy tried to sleep, and sleep would not come. Her head was resting on her own feather pillow, and she was safe in her own home. There was no need for her to fret, but something was wrong.

Yes, it was Spring. The time of LIFE. The time to put plants into the earth and to HOPE. But it was Spring that marked the loss of her own babies. And that pink dogwood was still screaming about DEATH!

"I'll not lie here one more minute, not one more! By thunder, I'm up. God he'p me to know what to do with myse'f."

As she dressed herself, she could hear Nellie in the kitchen. *She'll need help to feed the men.* So Bitsy marched herself to the back of the house, and passed the room with the closed door. She had all together ceased going into the room, choosing to stand outside the door where the pain of emptiness couldn't reach her. There was no cradle or child's bed—just a chifferobe.

None of their babies had ever been in that room. There was only dust and a closed trunk—full of baby things, full of empty hope and broken promises.

It was after the two women had fed the workers, washed the dishes, and sat down to talk that Bitsy told on herself: "All night long I werried myse'f 'bout that room. Truth is ... I've been wantin' a baby that h'ain't come. Ten years of hopin' an' wres'lin' with what to do with myse'f. Nellie, thar's a sick boy needs keerin' fer. An' I got a room what's been beggin' fer a little life to come fill h'it up. I'm so silly! What's to keep me from keerin' fer him? Till we git some answers, h'it looks like God has picked me fer the job. But what will Wick say?" That question had kept her awake, too. He got so silent when he caught her standing in front of that door. She remembered that Spring was painful to him, too.

Eager Nellie was already up and gathering supplies for cleaning. As they wiped their tears away and walked to that door, they both had a good laugh! Nellie opened the door first, went straight for the window, turned, and made her announcement.

"Now you listen to me, Betsy Miller! This whole mountain is behind y'uns. Wick'll be fine with the boy. It was Sister Downs' idee ta send me, not fer he'pin' with them men, ner did she send me to he'p you. I'm here fer the boy. So let's git ta warshin' and scrubbin'. They'll be here sometime t'day."

Two brooms. Two women. Two buckets of water. Two sets of hands to scrub. Two very determined women who knew how to value what they had and knew, and more importantly, they knew how to share anything, including their knowledge, with someone who seemingly had nothing. With pride and gratefulness, they scrubbed the inside of the room while it clouded outside and occasionally thundered. Rain was promised. And while the rain held off, Bitsy and Nellie made multiple trips to the barn. It was clear that Wick had purposely hidden the furniture from Bitsy and himself. Nellie didn't mention how long the things had been in the barn nor did she make conversation about how much water it was taking to clean everything. It was pointless to bring up the babies. Spring was already telling them all what was going to happen next.

Bitsy asked herself about the possibility of hurt. *Am I strong 'nough for this testin'? What if the boy didn't make it? What if there was nothin' any of us could do ta he'p? What if it turned out like it did with my babies?* She carried them in her womb right up until the last, expecting to see a face that had eyes that were alive—expecting to hear a cry to announce a desire to live … to belong … to her and to Wick … for all eternity.

Brother Bill caught Nellie and Bitsy sitting down. But it was evident that they had not been resting on their laurels—especially with the dirt smudges on both their faces and their hair coming unplaited. He fixed his own dinner plate, and he poured his own coffee. And then he waited for one of them to open their mouths.

As Brother Bill was finishing his coffee, Nellie spoke. "Brother Bill, we thank it's a fine and right decision ta brang the boy here fer the time bein'. It'll free up Doc ta do his job and with Wick hur, Bitsy can manage ever thang. I kin stay a day, maybe two. They won't need a thang and the boy just needs peace and quiet—like Doc said." It was indeed obvious what those two women had been up to; he didn't need any more clues.

23

Two Boys

The wind began to make a fuss as Wick steered Timmy and the wagon towards the mill. His stomach hurt from the stress and worrying. "Lord, hold back the rain till we git shelter. Thank ye." But the pray-er was not satisfied to leave off the worrying. He looked back at the boy on the travelling bed in the wagon and tried to get a clear reading from Doc's eyes. He couldn't tell if things were all right. There was only more road in front of them and a decision to make. He was going to chance hurrying. Timmy had been well looked-after while he was tied up near the chapel and Wick hoped and prayed that the horse would be willing to quicken the pace.

The journey was uphill the whole way—and quite steep in places. Yet Timmy was eager to hurry home. Wick had decided that unless Doc insisted that they take it easy, the troop was going to make a run for home. It was thundering and flashes of lightning were evidence of that storm Sister Downs was expecting. The wind seemed to produce the wings to help them get there faster.

The road to the Miller's place began at the fork just below the passage to Founder's Tree. The gentle incline was easily managed and wide enough for a full-sized wagon and a man on horse to pass at the same time. The Miller's homestead had a simple structure with notched logs as its living quarters. There were two small barns for livestock and equipment. Their homestead included livestock and necessary gardens. The only thing different from most home sites on that mountain was its simple wooden waterwheel that took advantage of downhill flowing water to power its grinding stone.

The crewmen working on clearing the tree that had fallen in the last storm were coming down from Founder's Tree as the familiar Miller's wagon was coming up the mountain road. Each member of the crew could feel the urgency of life and had been praying for the boy. This wagon was evidently carrying the boy to shelter. These men knew the surgery had saved his life, and they became energized to become a part of keeping that little life going. That wagon was on a mission, like an arrow to a target—and so were they!

Brother Downs, with his pipe in his teeth, hollered for the women to get ready. They were home. Somehow Doc and Wick knew that the best thing to do for the boy was to bring him to the mill. And they knew Bitsy was going to be a part of his complete healing. The boy had arrived, and the whole mill seemed to be singing its own genuine welcome. Nellie was the first one out to greet Doc and his patient as Wick was giving instructions to every man present.

"Boys, let's git this food to the kitchen afore hit gits wet. And two of y'uns can he'p Doc an' me git the boy settled." Words were spoken calmly and clearly. The wind was tearing at the quilts and blowing the hay into their faces causing Doc to cover the boy like a hen sheltering her chicks.

None of them seemed to notice the wind but went right on hauling food, quilts, equipment, and anything else Wick handed them.

Bitsy was waiting in the room and orchestrating the comings and goings of the helpers. She was helping life.

Doc Williams stepped over the side of the wagon and made his directions clear and concise. "We're gonna use that feather bed like a stretcher. Men, each of yuns get a tight grip on a co'ner. We'll slide him off that hay and carry 'im to Bitsy. She'll know what to do then. Gentle like, gentle ..."

Brother Bill, Nellie, and Bitsy had spent the last hours putting the ropes into the antique bed frame found in the barn. Bitsy had never seen the bed before, but nobody had time for questions. It was truly a blessing that all the pieces of the bed were found, and it was bigger than a baby's crib. The boy would have a proper place to rest and heal.

Four men brought the boy in, and ever-so-gently, they lowered that little human frame on to that old bed frame. The fresh straw-filled mattress cradled the invalid. And, as they all held their breath, the doctor examined the boy. "We've made it, thank ye, God. Praise be ta God." And then the unexpected happened: Doc Williams began to cry. He sank to the floor while the tears spilled down his cheeks. There was no stopping the emotion that leaped out of this man. His shoulders shook and very little sound escaped his lips.

And then Doc let out a sigh—a sigh of relief. Sensible Nellie silently stood beside the doctor and waited. Everyone else in the room had bowed their heads in honor of him, showing the respect he deserved. And when he stood, she lovingly guided him out of the room. He needed to be taken care of, and she was the one—the only one—he would permit to care for him in that way.

The crewmen excused themselves and hurried to the barn ahead of the approaching rain. It was in a hushed kitchen that Brother Bill assisted the women in preparing a cold supper for the men in the barn. He quietly considered the exhaustion that had overcome the doctor and prayed for healing sleep to come to both Wick and Doc. Once the basket was filled, he excused himself from the kitchen for the night. As he stepped out into the dark with the basket of vittles in one hand, Brother Bill discretely closed the door of the house with the other hand. He lifted his face toward heaven and asked, "Peace to all that's in that house, Lord. Please bring yer peace and strength to 'em all. Amen."

The clouds could not hold back the water any longer. Gentle rain drops fell at first making a "hush" sound. And as it got steadier and the drops got heavier, they silenced all other noises. There it was, like Sister Downs said, a Spring rain—needed rain—life-giving rain. Water for the soul of the Earth, cleansing in its nature. If ever there was a need for rain, it was that night. For nothing compares to the rest-giving sleep received from a night of gentle rain.

The moon was hidden by the water clouds, but Wick's face and body hid nothing. He was spent, and it was Bitsy's delight to send Wick to bed, for once—a definite reversal of roles. Their baths could wait until tomorrow.

Wick finally sat down on his side of their bed. Bitsy removed his shoes and socks. Then she lifted the covers and down he lay. His eyes closed before his head touched the pillow. But the look of his handsome face was different. "I'll be close by, dearest. Everything is taken care of, I promise." Walking towards that other room felt natural. Finally.

Bitsy took up her post as she planted herself on a chair. The boy was breathing steadily and gently. Like the rain. He looked so small. She wanted to guess his age, but she felt strongly that her guess would be wrong. She wanted to know his name, but what if he couldn't remember it? That happened sometimes when there's been a high fever or not enough nourishment to keep the brain alive. He was so thin. Bitsy wondered, *How could his parents let t'at happen?*

"I mussn't get worked up 'bout thangs," she said outloud. "God got him this fer. He'll do what's right by the chile." So, to keep her mind from wandering, she began to write down the details of all the events that involved this little boy. If he could not remember, she had her part written down.

Tomorrow she would write down Wick's and Doc's recollection of events. Rosie's account would have to wait until the right time. And she could add Brother Bill Downs to this list of important participants. And dear sweet Nellie Weathers.

24

The Help

In the very next room, Wick slept soundly in his own bed for the first time in almost a week. Doc Williams had landed on the pallet of quilts and goose down that Nellie had arranged for him. Bitsy was thinking how good it would be if all three could sleep for at least one whole day undisturbed.

If the child could sleep like he was sleeping just then for an entire week, it would give them all confidence that healing was taking place. This child needed comfort and peace. Bitsy had so many questions for him—questions about him and because of him. The questions alone formed a mountain that she could not get her mind around or over. She felt strained under the weight of emotion produced by having to wait on answers.

In the silence of the dimly lit room, Bitsy rehearsed her conversations should the boy wake up.

"Howdy, my name is Betsy Miller. What's yourn?"

What if he asked whar he was?

"Chile, yer stayin' with us til yer well enuff to go home."

What if he wanted to know what was wrong with him or why he was in a stranger's bed?

"I'll jest tell 'im he got sick and a doctor took keer of 'im. And that hit'll be alright. An' I ain't gonna leave him."

Why had she said that? She was not going to leave him. He would be leavin' her. When he was well.

There was an endless string of conversations that came to her mind. Bitsy was realizing that she didn't have any way of knowing just what to expect next. The little woman who was on watch that night was slowly surrendering to the will of her Heavenly Father.

She put away her pencil and paper. It was not time for that, yet. A cool wind was pushing the rain against the window panes forcing her to look for her shawl. "That wind is blowin' cold right through them cracks!" She reached her small hand towards the quiet child in the bed. "He'll need more keevers."

She silently moved through the room, this time humming to herself. Bitsy stood in front of the child-size chiffarobe, where she and Nellie had moved all the beautiful baby things. Without pausing, or considering the past, she retrieved a small blanket. *My, how small 'his blanket is … but he won't notice hit was fer a baby. My, but ain't he small.* She stopped and placed her hand on his chest. There it was beating strong, working to heal that weak body. A lump came to her throat.

His Mama must be sick herse'f from werrin' bout him. Goodness knows how long they've been lookin' fer 'im. Oh, God he'p that Mama know he's all right, now. Bitsy sat back down to pray and to watch. And that is how the hours ticked by, little by little, and with the realization that she was the one being comforted as she watched the boy breathe.

Nellie was trying her best not to make any noise the next morning. She had successfully milked the cow without disturbing anyone and had fed the men in the barn. It was still raining and they were sleeping in, too. Brother Bill came to help her in the kitchen. "Mable don't let me he'p much. In the kitchen, that is. She says I break too many dishes and I'm best at he'pin' tote water and peelin' the taters. So LET ME AT 'EM!"

There was no door to close to keep noises from drifting toward the bedrooms. Nellie was frustrated. She didn't want any help, especially if it meant more noise. Last night Wick and Doc looked worn, and their faces were telling her how much they had sacrificed for the little boy. She meant to give them a chance to sleep. Her solution was to send Brother Bill to the grinding room that was connected to the kitchen. He was glad to go and was all smiles as he carried the burlap sack of potatoes and made his way to work on helping Nellie with breakfast. Or, maybe it was going to become lunch?

Nellie put the coffee on to boil. It was half past 11 in the morning.

She scooted the rocking chair closer to the stove. "Sure is cool this mornin'. I hope them two men had enough keevers. I hope Bitsy had sense ta git out some a them baby thangs." Nellie didn't have a husband or any children. But she took care of lots of people. She had a sense—a knowing about her. She would just show up. To help. But she never overstayed her welcome.

It was Doc Williams who showed his face in the kitchen first. "Just need my coffee, if ye please, Miss Nellie." She was already pouring it up. "Black, jest like Brother Bill drinks his." He was looking for a chair. "Have ye seen Bitsy yet? I was hopin' the boy was still sleepin'. Thank God fer that bed last night.

"Ye can thank God but hit 'twas me that thunk of it, an' I'm a thankin' h'its time fer yer bath. Brother Bill's got it all squared away in the barn. I'll have yer vittles ready afore too long. Now, let me pour ye a hot cup full so's ye can enjoy it with yer bath." Nellie had him all figured out. Doc Williams could only grin back at her. "Thank ye, ma'm."

Her menu was fried potato hash with browned sausage. Gravy and biscuits. Bacon and fried apples. Johnny cakes with jam and maple syrup. And fresh buttermilk.

Who's to say which smell got to Wick first. He was up and in the kitchen, and Nellie had to fight him off with a wooden spoon. No one wanted to wake the boy, so Wick surrendered, willingly. She quelled his hunger with a fresh cup of coffee, and then sent him to the barn for bathing.

The smell of that wonderful food was wafting under the door to the room where the boy had been sleeping and Bitsy had stood watch through the night. Bitsy took the smells as a signal from Nellie that relief was on the way. There had been no changes in the boy. But as Bitsy rose to open the door, she heard a noise. It was coming from the bed. The boy was stirring and making noises, but the sounds were mixed with mumbling. "Mama, it hurts, it hurts som'thin' awful … ow …" He was trying to breathe.

"I'm here, son. Jest a minute." Before Bitsy could get herself back to his side, in came Nellie. "He'p me hold his hands. We don't need them stitches ta be torn loose." The women quickly got his flailing arms under control. "Mama, he'p me." His eyelids were squeezed shut because of the pain.

Bitsy tried to talk, but he was still fighting back. They waited it out. He finally settled down and began breathing normally. Nellie stayed on one side of the bed and steadied herself for another round of wrestling. Bitsy stood on the other watching that little face.

After a few minutes, Nellie slipped out and headed straight for the kitchen. Bitsy could hear the men's voices, and she could tell Nellie was giving her report. Bitsy got out her paper and pencil to write down the event for the doctor's records.

"Mama, I'm hungry," the boy said faintly.

What was that? Was it the boy? Bitsy did not dare move too quickly. She lifted her head to look at his face. His eyes were still closed. "Wake up, son. Wake up."

"I'm tryin' … my head's a hurtin' an … they feel so heavy."

Bitsy was almost whispering. "Keep tryin'." She got a wet cloth. "I'll he'p 'em some," wiping gently, "Thar. Try openin' 'em one more time." She was leaning over him, waiting to see all of his face.

"I was dreamin' of apple pie. An' bacon." His eyelids were still shut tight.

"You jest keep dreamin' and sleepin'." It was then that Bitsy realized just why this boy was so small. She went weak in the knees forcing her to be seated quickly. She couldn't breathe. Her motherly instincts had just kicked her in the stomach. *He had been neglected— starved!* Bitsy violently covered her face with her apron and ran out of the room so that he couldn't hear her crying.

It was impossible not to hear those sounds of sobbing. Wick and Doc were most definitely moved, but they went right past Bitsy and straight away entered the room startled to see the boy sitting, propped up by his elbows and forearms. He looked wild-eyed with fright.

Doc recognized the boy's state of mind. Quiet words were then spoken to him. "Come, come now, son. Nobody's gonna hurt ya."

Wick interjected, "I was the one that carried ye to the doctor," he said pointing to Doc. There was still no sound from the boy's mouth and no change in his body language. His eyes were fixed on them and his little fingers were squeezed around the quilt that covered his lap. "My name is Wick Miller. This is my house. This is Doc Williams."

The boy's eyes were darting from face to face. He was unsure and still frightened.

Both men stopped their advancement. They were stuck, glued to the floor right where they stood. They could see irrational fear written all over this boy. "We'll stay right chere. No need to upset ye. E're ye hungry? Nellie's cooked a fine … "

In mid-sentence Doc stopped, realizing the boy was shaking and his head was bobbing and before anyone could blink, he passed out, falling back on the pillow.

How their feet came instantly unglued! They both rushed the bed, Doc patting the boys hands and face, Wick hovering.

"Git my bag," Doc said. Wick handed it to him quickly. Doc fished out a bottle, pulled its stopper and ran it under the boy's nose.

"Can ye hear me? Son, can ye hear me? Come back, come back, now."

Wick was gripping the wood post of the bed, praying under his breath.

Sometime during the commotion, Bitsy and Nellie had squeezed together at the foot of the bed, holding hands and praying silently.

The boy stirred again, his eyelids fluttered and then stayed opened. And they settled on Bitsy's face.

"Howdy, I'm Bitsy. What's yer name?"

"Thomas."

"Ya've bin sick and we all bin takin' keer of ye. E're ye ready ta eat?"

"Yes'm."

Nellie slid quietly out of the room with Wick following her to the kitchen.

"I'm Doc Williams. How old 'ere ye, Thomas?"

"Eight, I think."

Doc's skilled hands were checking out the real physical condition of this small eight-year-old boy named Thomas. Doc proceeded to cautiously examine the boy. "Son, ya've been sick, nearly died, truth be tole, but we got out the infection. See hur." He took out a mirror to show him the sutures. "Now hit's all better." Then Doc asked Bitsy for the healing salve in his bag, Thomas could only blink and stare at the mirror, trying his best to understand.

"We couldn't leave the pizen in thar ... hit would'a kilt ye."

Thomas was silent. He was remembering a nightmare he recently had.

"My head hurts. Whar's the well? I gotta fetch me some water. I'm awful thirsty." He was desperately struggling to raise himself to get out of the bed.

"Hold on, Thomas!" It was Wick. "I got us a fresh pail a water an' ye can drink all ye want. Right thar in the bed."

Doc looked down into Thomas's face confirming the command to stay in bed.

"Wick'll carry ye to the privy. Til ye git yer own stren'th back. Maybe a day or two. Maybe."

Bitsy had again taken up her post on the chair beside the bed, listening and waiting. And closely watching Thomas drink fresh water from the dipper. He was still shaking but awake now. Wick was helping to hold the dipper steady to avoid spills.

In her soft, gentle voice she spoke to him.

"Now, I know yer not a baby no more, but if'n you'll let Nellie feed ye, hit won't tire ye out so."

She so wanted to touch him in a reassuring way. But the look on Thomas's face told her ... not yet. So she surrendered her chair to Nellie who was then bringing him his food.

The two men were still squeezed together at the foot of the bed watching Thomas. Wick then said, "Doc says ye can eat what ye like, but a little at the time. So what'll it be? Fried apples an' biscuits? I buttered 'em ... hot and ready when you ere."

Thomas's face looked like he wanted to cry. And then it changed to a frown, and doubt and a wrinkled forehead. "Don't I have ta do chores afore I kin et?" He asked, genuinely.

Wick spoke, almost shouted. His words broke something in the air around Thomas's head. "Not while yer in my home." He quieted down, pleading for understanding. "God has give me plenty a stren'th ta do what needs doin'. Yer ta git well so's we kin git ye home."

Nellie had already put a fork full of apples into Thomas's mouth and had that hot buttered biscuit ready when that had gone down. Thomas was weakly chewing, with his eyes closed.

"Let's let him alone ta enjoy his food." Bitsy defended.

"Yes'm, I'd like ta see what he does with this cup a cold milk." Nellie chimed in.

And down went the mouthful of biscuit followed by the entire cup of cold milk. All of it with Thomas's eyes still closed. It seemed that was all he could handle. He then slept.

Doc had motioned for Nellie to follow him. Once they were in the kitchen he gave her a package of herbs, told her how to prepare them, and when to administer them. Doc then said, "Providence has made it clear, this boy's gonna make hit. But we gotta be keerful ta git his stren'th back. What happens next'll either make him a strong man … or hit'll make him a weaklin' the rest a his days."

She nodded. She more than understood all the dimensions to the care of this boy. What's more, she knew Bitsy and Wick could and would do what was right.

25

The Barn

No more rain fell during the night, and the clear morning sent the clearing crew back to their chores at home. Founder's Pass was open again, though its landscape was forever changed.

Doc was gone, too. A fast horse brought a messenger to the mill during the night. Time to move on to the next case. And away he had ridden before the sun had risen and before Nellie could fix him a proper breakfast.

So Wick, Brother Bill Downs, and Nellie met again in the Miller's kitchen, and the topic of discussion of course was Thomas and what to do next. He had spent the remainder of the previous day eating and sleeping. Bitsy and Nellie had been taking turns watching over him and feeding him.

Thomas seemed guarded still, and all of the adults considered the circumstances that had gotten him to that point. They each filled in the blanks as Thomas had not divulged any secrets. Bitsy was resolved to focus on the task of getting the child well, well enough to return to his parents. They all agreed on that point.

Later that afternoon, while Thomas still slept soundly, Wick helped Brother Bill and Nellie get their things gathered so they could also return to their homes.

Brother Bill then said, "Nellie and I have done jest about all we kin fer now. She told Bitsy what to do with the herbs. Them two have a secret understandin'. Always have. Doc will have to come check on the boy, Thomas, I mean, and he'll let us know if'n we're needed."

Wick knew the truth had just been spoken. So he and Bitsy waved good-bye to their two friends who had been so faithful and helpful. Wick watched them ride down that same road that had brought

Thomas to the mill. Bitsy had immediately taken up her post so as not to leave Thomas alone.

Bitsy wrote more notes for the doctor to read when he returned. She watched Thomas breathe in and out. She read her Bible. She re-read the story of Hannah—the Hannah who petitioned the Lord for a child and promised to return him to God at the appointed time. It was her personal story of HOPE.

Bitsy was forced to surrender her babies. She wasn't given a choice. She read further in the scriptures that Hannah took care of Samuel until it was time to send him to do what God and she had agreed upon. She had many long talks with her God about her babies—Wick's children. She was resolved. If Hannah could do it, so could she. After all, it was written that God heard Hannah's cry. Thomas lying under the baby quilt in her home was proof of God's love for Betsy Miller. She had cried out to God to save his little life. He loved her no less than He loved Hannah. When she looked over Thomas's face, she thanked God Almighty for sparing his life—and for using her and Wick to help save him.

Wick had drawn plenty of water for Thomas to drink, and plenty was drawn from the creek to do the dish washing. The coffee and the rain barrels were spilling over. Wick had no need to prepare any food as Nellie had taken care of that. So the next item was to straighten out the barn. Myrtle was let out with the cow into the pin to give him room to work. He was grateful for the quiet opportunity to think and consider what had happened, and to ponder what was to be done when Thomas remembered where his home was. But Wick was getting ahead of himself.

He had not told Bitsy what had happened to him in the chapel graveyard. And he knew that he had to tell her. He began rehearsing the conversation in his mind as he was scrubbing out the bathing tub. The analogy running through his mind was intriguing and funny at the same time. He was "washing" the tub and remembering his "washing" in the graveyard. The thoughts produced real laughter, right in that barn.

Miracles happened fer me and fer Thomas. I'm thankful to ye, Lord. An' I'll say thank ye fer Thomas. He'll say it hisse'f real soon, I'm sure. So will his folks. Amen.

With chores comes singing and whistling, and for Myrtle and the cow, a clean barn. One that did not have to be shared with a bunch of strangers.

Two bright blue birds settled on the fence rail. Two mountain blue birds. Their beauty and friendliness contrasted with the chilly air. Warm or cold, Spring had arrived—along with the blue birds. As the sun was setting, Wick put away his tools. Walking right past the birds, Wick then carried the bathing tub into the house, and placed it in front of the fireplace in the main room. Bitsy would want a bath later, so he started a fire to help with the chill and to heat the water. He wanted dinner first, and then he would take over with Thomas. He had never fed a baby before—much less a grown child. It had to be done.

"Wick, Thomas is asleep now an' I'm too tired ta eat. I'm goin' ta bed. You call me if'n ye need me. I mean it."

"I need ta tell ye somethin' Bitsy. But I want ye ta rest an' when ye wake, I'll tell it. You'll be fresh that a way."

She was already under the covers. He pulled the door shut. And made his way to the kitchen to fix his food, which was eaten in peace. He prepared a bowl for Thomas, and he made his way to the chair beside him. It was difficult waking the boy for the necessary trip to the privy. Wick scooped Thomas up. He was so light. They must get some meat on his bones. Thomas kept his eyes closed as they traveled to the outhouse. He didn't respond to Wick's questions, which made Wick worry about the child's hearing. When everything was accomplished, Wick brought him back and helped him wash up.

"Whar is she? Thomas asked.

"Do ye mean Bitsy? Or Nellie?" Wick said as he was feeding Thomas venison stew. "Nellie makes a tasty venison stew but Bitsy's ain't nothin' ta sneeze at."

"Bitsy."

"She's takin' a little rest so she can be with ye later. Us men can git along without her fer a spell, cain't we?"

"I wanted ta tell her sumpin'.

"I see. Why don't ye rest some more an' tell her later. I got somethin' I need ta tell her myse'f.

26

The Shout

The Evil Accuser was relaxed and seated around the Cauldron's fire. REJECTION and ABANDONMENT had shouted their victories and praised themselves over how well their strategies had affected the boy's life. Boistrous and gutteral proclamations rang through the trees, and across the Cauldron's climbing flames danced HUNGER and DISAPPOINTMENT in a drunken triumphant dance. Each boast was batted and thrown around and overpowered the atmosphere with evil. Each spirit felt it was the winner of this game of DEATH and destruction.

But it was LOVE that made an announcement, a declaration so strong and defiant it shattered the spirits' confidence. Instead, the lie of all lies, that king of titles worn by numerous humans on Earth, the UNLOVED name was about to be dethroned by UNCONDITIONAL LOVE. The Accuser had been discovered as the source of all Thomas's sufferings.

Black was the Cauldron that had been filled, and yet its liquid vaporized before it hit the ground. SUFFERING stood watching, waiting for instructions. It got none. Each member of this life-destroying team was dumbfounded. A great and fearful LIGHT pressed down on them with such TRUTH that they all were silenced. And fearful. This LIGHT cut them with joyful fingers—fingers that gripped around the throat of DESPAIR and HUNGER, refusing to relent. And then, they were all pierced with such violence that all were silenced. LOVE would leave no survivors here.

Each had plotted and executed their best plans as pawns in the serious game of LIFE and DEATH. All of the strategies to destroy the LIFE of Thomas were now shattered by HOPE!

Thomas slept in a bed of warmth and ease, but his mind could not rest. The poison had tried to take his life for sure, and with that fight for LIFE came the relentless nightmares that only fevers can feed. But the ringing in his ears was the most unbearable.

While his head was lying still on his pillow, painful sounds came. But this ringing in his ears came not from a hideous creature of the dream world, but from a memory. His Mama's voice came to him like a ringing.

"Thomas, never lie, especially to yerse'f."

He could not escape the hurt. He knew he had been spared; the stitches would be a reminder for the rest of his life on Earth. Slowly he was remembering how he had gotten into this strange bed. Piece by peace, he was managing the truth of his own personal tragedy, which included the pitiful reminder that he had been forced to endure abuses because all those days had been days without Mama.

This stranger and his wife would have to hear it from his own lips. He had to tell them the truth. He would not endure the suffering that silence brought—not for one more day or one more night.

Thomas turned over in the bed. He was gathering the courage to look the man in the eyes. He lacked confidence. Hadn't the past taught him anything? Do what you're told and don't ask for anything. It was much safer when he took instructions and expected a beating. His heart screamed to be heard so with trembling voice he said, "Hey, Mister. Could I have a drink a water? An' would ye please git her. I cain't wait no longer." Such a serious look reflected on both their faces.

"Yes. I'll go now."

Wick handed Thomas the dipper and waited to return it to the bucket. Then he all but ran to get Bitsy, praying the little woman would be able to hear what the boy had to say. He was also praying that he would be able to hear what the boy had to say. His heart was heavy in his chest, and emotion was creeping up his throat.

He quietly opened the door and called her name. "Bitsy, yer needed." To his surprise she was already out of bed, dressed in a fresh skirt and tying on her shoes.

"He needs ta tell ye somethin'. I ain't sure what but hits kept him from sleepin'. Maybe he's homesick but don't 'member how ta git home, oh, I don't know. Come on."

Bitsy was out the door, and Wick was stepping right behind her. They hadn't had their talk. It would have to wait. She went to the chair. He pulled up a stool beside her, intent on hearing every word Thomas said.

"Good evenin', Thomas. Have ye slept good?"

"Naw, I h'aint. I need ta tell yuns sumpin' … I run away … BUT I CAIN'T GO BACK."

They were blinking with this new information.

"But yer Maw and Paw will be a missin' ye, son. Hit t'weren't that bad, were it?"

Now, Wick had seen the scars on Thomas's body. He knew there was something wrong from the beginning.

"That's what I'm tryin' ta tell ye. I h'aint got no Mama, no more." He was beginning to cry. "She died. She died." His sobs were taking over his words. "I h'aint never gonna see her again. 'Til Heaven."

They were all crying by this time, and Thomas kept right on talking through his tears and pain.

"I was gived away the day after Mama went into the ground. An' I was taken fur away. I t'weren't loved no more. That's the truth."

He was wiping his nose and face on the quilt he had been pounding just before.

Bitsy was crying so hard by then she was shaking and wiping her own nose and face on her skirt. Wick was in so much pain, he could no longer look the boy in the face.

It was silent for a time.

"Who was it took ye in? Whar did ye come from?" Wick had gained some of his composure back.

"T'weren't no takin' me in. I wuz traded fer a horse. That was the only secret Clifton ever tole me. His woman, Viney, told me plenty how I were 'bout as useful as that lame horse I got traded fer."

Bitsy crumpled into the floor, unable to keep her sobs quiet. Wick wasn't sitting on the stool anymore. He was pounding his fist into his other hand subconsciously pulverizing an unknown enemy repeatedly while his mind was spinning with all the inferences Thomas's speech made.

Thomas exhaled in the silence. His eyes were still wet with tears and he had turned his face opposite Bitsy and Wick's faces. They would have to deal with his truth telling. He was cleaned of any guilt from having harbored the truth of his previous life. It was the truth!

Yes, HOPE was in the room with them. It was Wick's turn to tell the truth. Bitsy had finally gained strength enough to be seated again. Her mouth opened and shut three times. There were no words capable of expressing her emotions. Her hands lay idly on her lap, her head bowed.

"Thomas, Bitsy ... I gotta tell yuns 'bout that night."

He waited to see if Thomas would look his direction.

"While you was feverish an' Doc and Rosie was havin' ta fight fer yer life, I was fightin' with God 'bout the past. I wanted you ta live ... ever'body needs new chances ... at livin'.... even the ones that h'aint even sick. I had ta ask God ta furgive me fur my bein' angry at Him. An' Bitsy, Darlin', will ye furgive me fur not hopin' with ye 'bout chil'ren? An' fer bein' cross with ye? God loves us, all. He wants us ta love Him, no matter what."

His words came as more of a pleading than questions or requests. He had been close-fisted and spoke with a definite lump in his throat. Ever-so-slowly, he took a breath in and while he let out his breath, he turned his face to look down at Bitsy.

Bitsy was overcome by this confession and could only whisper her forgiveness. There would be no reward in staying hurt with that man. It was altogether real, this change of heart.

TIME was on their side, again. Their common wounds inflicted by DEATH were now receiving a permanent HEALING. Through this sweet forgiveness, HEALING was coming from Heaven and from Earth. And HEALING was

the rich reward of UNCONDITIONAL LOVE. Wick finally rested his hand on the tiny shoulders that had carried his hurts for so long.

Thomas was looking at Bitsy, looking at Wick, and wondering what was going to happen to himself. He had never heard such language before. The whole scene seemed like a lie, but all he could do was let their honest tears prove to him that LOVE was invited to live at this house. So was HOPE.

But the real question in Thomas's mind was there to be any HOPE for him here?

Bitsy stretched her hand towards the bed. It rested on Thomas's leg. Her eyes were searching his face to know what to do or say next.

Thomas lay down on the bed. It was apparent how much this truth-telling cost him physically. Bitsy kept her hand close by waiting for the right time to speak. His eyes were still opened.

Wick moved his stool close to the head of the bed, close to Bitsy's chair.

They made room for Thomas to tell them what was on his heart. He looked so small lying there in that room. Oh, he was not the baby they had been expecting … and yet he seemed like an infant in his need for nurturing, protecting, and loving.

All were silent. It was a natural waiting. Bitsy and Wick Miller knew a lot about waiting.

As the sun was setting, Thomas closed his eyes and tried to speak. He didn't have the strength. Bitsy was moved by Wick's confession and the facts that Thomas had laid at their door. It was finally her turn to speak.

"Thomas, thar's nuttin' ta werry 'bout ta night. Wick an me'll be right chere, no matter what time hit is. A waitin' ta listen ta whatever ye want ta tell us."

Precious, beautiful QUIET filled the room. Darkness settled in and was welcomed. LOVE sat on the stool with HOPE next to it on the chair. They were joined. By two humans, a man and his wife, each willing to take up their post. Keeping vigil over this blessing of LIFE.

Wick moved respectfully to light the oil lamp on top of the chifferobe, turning its wick down to soften the edges of the dark. It was Bitsy who almost absent-mindedly hummed a tune, to which Wick gave words with his rich voice:

"My Jesus I love Thee, I know Thou art mine;
For Thee all the follies of sin I resign;
My gracious redeemer, my Savior art Thou;
If ever I loved Thee my Jesus tis now.
I love Thee because Thou hast first loved me;
And purchased my pardon on Calvary's tree;
I love Thee for wearing the thorns on Thy brow;
If ever I loved Thee, my Jesus tis now.
In mansions of glory and endless delight;
I'll ever adore Thee in Heaven so bright;
I'll sing with the glittering crowns on my brow;
If every I loved Thee, my Jesus tis now."[3]

27

Name Calling

LOVE is a beauty. HOPE is a stream. FORGIVENSS brings new LIFE. All keep vigil over the heart. Precious is LIFE. Learn from the Father. He brings LIGHT from above. MORNNG is His proof.

Thomas woke with the coming of the sun. And this rising sun was introduced by a soon-to-be famous rooster. That thunderous announcement forced him to jump out of his bed. Thomas's feet produced a loud thud as they landed on the floor while he struggled to manage his upper body. He naturally grabbed his side that was stinging and keeping him from straightening up. And there was no one around to assist him. He was forced to fall backwards onto his bed and wait out the stabbing pain.

In an instant, both Wick and Bitsy were at his side. They had heard both his feet hit the floor and his declaration of pain. So this was to be his first day—of starting over.

"Whoa, boy. Let me he'p ye. Think ye can walk to the outhouse? I think ye otta try hit. I'll be right behine ye." Thomas was still biting his lip as Bitsy helped him to sit up. Wick was impressed that Thomas had not cried one tear despite his pain.

"That dumb rooster nearly got me kilt ... I furgot whar I was ... I guess I was headed to do my chores." Thomas knew then how much strength he had lost because his head was spinning. "I'll try standin' first." It was more like a rocking first attempt, but he was determined. He hated being in bed all the time.

Bitsy needed to check on his stitches before anything else happened. "You fellers do what needs doin'. I've got food ready. May be that t'morry we could bring us a table and chur in hur an' eat proper?"

Wick was too focused to have heard anything she had said. Thomas was not very steady on his feet—he was so unsteady that he did not make it out of the bedroom before Wick had to catch him. The look on Thomas's face showed how disappointed he was in himself. Wick struggled to keep a solemn face.

"Not too bad fer yer first day, by gum. Let's git our mornin' started an' have some vittles."

Washed hands, washed faces. Clean plates, clean forks. Happy birds were chirping back and forth to each other with the sound of the creek rushing past the big wheel outside the grinding room. *Thay's no end to the new sights and sounds hur at 'his place*, Thomas thought. But he had lots of questions about the things that had gone on while he was sick. *But will they tell me the truth?* He was so unsure. They seemed like honest people, but he quivered inside when he considered what kind of people he had just left behind him. Words would not be used to describe those animals. If he could just do something—some difficult job—maybe these people—the Millers—would show their true colors. But then it came back to him what the man had said about his own strength coming from God and the doctor insisting that he save his strength. To get well. To go home.

That word used to mean Mama and Brooks and Baby Toy and Margaret and of course Ross and Ralph. Where were they now? What did they look like? Who, if anybody, was feeding and giving them a "room"? Thomas was remembering that dark morning when he left the cabin, alone. He was remembering that first day without Mama. He could not let himself be happy—even all this time later. Oh, his breakfast was tasty, and the two adults ate together, at the same time, at the same table. But how could he trust one scene? Truth be told, he had never seen his Mama eat a meal with his father at the same table. Father ate alone. He couldn't remember seeing Mama eat at the table. Mama ran them out of the house whenever father was around. Ralph and Ross had to keep the babies quiet. Why? Why had he remembered that worried face that Mama had when the babies cried?

She had told them all that, "Werryin' makes ye old," Funny, he hadn't thought about that until just now.

Bet I look as old as dirt.

It must have been that his thoughts were written all over his face because Bitsy kept looking at him. And she was writing on her papers.

"Thomas, what is yer whole name?"

Why did she want to know that? He felt like he was being looked at from the inside out.

"Thomas Alva … somethin' … c'ain't recall the rest." He shrugged his answer. "My brothers' names are Brooks, Ross, Ralph, Baby Toy. Gotta sister, too. Margaret." The names had spilled out of his mouth by accident. He thought, "thar ye go! Gone an' said too much."

She was writing down words, not really looking at his face anymore.

"Wonder what all that's fer?" he mumbled. Bitsy was sincerely focused on what she was writing down.

"What's yer daddy's name?" She waited for some time for his answer.

"I c'ain't 'member … only heard him called father. I steered clear a him. We all did." He clapped his hand over his mouth surprised at himself. Too much information.

Bitsy was writing that response down as well. She took a deep breath before asking the next question,

"An' yer Mama's name? Can ye remember it, Thomas?"

He had been lying in bed on his side, which was facing Bitsy in her chair. But he could not stand to look at her nor have her looking at him anymore.

She worried that he might not remember her name. What worried her more than that was that he knew it, but would not tell her. Instinctually Bitsy could tell that it had been his mother who had protected Thomas and he would still be protecting her memory. Bitsy would wait … and wait.

But he turned himself away from her, away from the open window with the sound of the babbling water in the creek and the chattering birds and the clean curtains fluttering in Spring's cool breeze.

The clock in the next room tick-tocked, tick-tocked, tick-tocked.

How long since he had said her name, had heard her name? He covered his head with the quilt. She had been covered with dirt …

That awful scene, under the oak tree with all of those strangers looking at them … looking at him. And he wanting only to look at Mama.

Gently he formed the words on his lips … with great respect and love came her name, whispered …

"Sarah Jane."

28

Scars

The very next day Doc Williams poked his head in the boy's room to see if his patient was doing alright. Wick had just seen Bitsy off on another call and was seated beside Thomas waiting for him to awaken. As Doc smiled his hello, he motioned his head for Wick to step out. Wick's heavy boots broke Thomas's sleep. With the door completely closed, the two men exchanged information out of earshot. But Thomas could hear the entire conversation. Stitches. He certainly would be happier without those bothersome thangs. They were itchy and poky. They would get caught on his nightshirt, on his under clothes, and make his nights miserable. He was all for getting rid of those things.

In short order, the two men stepped back into the room. It was Doc who confirmed the wonderful news. "Well, hit's time! Yur skin is all closed up and ya don't need them stitches anymore." Out came the scissors and the tweezers, and Wick brought the lamp close to his side.

Doc reminded Thomas that there was nothing he could not eat, and now he was telling him to eat all he wanted—all day long, if he wanted to. Thomas had not one inkling that such a thing was possible. *Eat all day? Eat all day?* The thought was too much to hold in his head.

"Ye mean, if I think 'bout bein' hungry, I jest ask fer food? Even when hit ain't meal time? Even if I h'ain't done no chores?" Thomas could not believe his ears.

Wick was still beside Doc helping with the removal of the dozens of threads in Thomas's side. He could not look him in the face just then, but he fully understood the child's dilemma.

"Thomas, Bitsy's gone ta help with birthin' so looks like you and me'll have ta fend fer ourse'ves. My cookin' ain't all that good. We both might end up skin an' bones." That was a picture Thomas could have laughed at, if he wasn't being aggravated by Doc's pulling and poking and pinching.

With all the commotion of Doc taking out his stitches, Thomas hadn't noticed that Bitsy was not around until Wick mentioned it. *What did he mean by that word "birthin"? How fur away was she? What was she doin'? And how long was she gonna be away? Had she left cause she was mad or somethin'?* Thomas wished Doc was finished.

The rooster was finishing his crowing about the new day as the doctor packed his bag. Wick returned the lamp to the beside and walked with Doc to the kitchen. Thomas swung his legs over the bed, planted his feet on the floor, and walked himself to the outhouse.

When Wick had confirmed that Thomas was out of earshot, he informed Doc of the earth-shattering truth about the boy. And he let him know of their suspicions. And without missing a word said or any thought inferred, Doc Williams revealed to Wick that what he had suspected all along was the exact thing that he had just been told.

"I knew he had been abused, starved, an' worked like an animal. God knows I felt hot anger 'bout what that boy had been through. Wick, you and Bitsy, you've gotta keep Thomas. Ye gotta keer fer him. T'ain't nobody else. I know hit!"

Wick bowed his head, mumbling something about being honored to do what he could. He moved then across the room, reaching into a bowl on the window shelf. Respectfully, he handled the bundle of papers Bitsy had tied and kept hidden in the kitchen. The words written there were meant for Doc Williams' eyes only.

It was time for Doc to go, but not before he gave Thomas specific instructions. "Keep that skin clean, and the scar needs salve on hit ever now an' then. Keeps it from itchin' and breakin' open in the thin spots."

Doc was out the door and mounting his horse as Thomas was approaching the stoop. He waved to the boy, but Thomas did not wave back. He was too worried about being alone with the man now standing in the kitchen doorway.

"Now there's some bad news," Wick said. "Yer gonna have ta take a bath. A real under-the-water-all-at-one-time kind. I hate it fer ye. But orders is orders. Hey, I know! You get warshed while I make biscuits. You'll find a surprise on yer bed. Might need ta investigate ... I dunno?"

Thomas was instructed on where the tub was and all of the gear that belonged to bathing. He still didn't like the feeling he had. While he was on his search for the gear, Wick was filling the bathing tub and adding a little log to the fire. He was then directed to get busy, because Wick was hungry.

"I'll go milk Fern, you do yer scrubbin', an' I'll be back ta fix the biscuits an' gravy." And out he went.

Thomas was still unsure of himself in these new surroundings, and he felt it would be better for him if he got the bathing over with. He remarked how long it had been since he had gotten a real under-the-water-all-at-one-time kind of bath. Too long. As he undressed, he made note of the clothes he was placing on the hearth. They were not his. Whose were they? Thoughtful and pensive was he as he cautiously stepped into the fancy tub. It was not made of wood but of metal, and the water had been carefully heated. Just right. He almost forgot the soap. He dunked the square soap under the water, which released its perfume. It smelled of honey and something else, which he did not recognize. He started at his feet and washed and scrubbed without thinking until he got to his scar. He would be ever so careful there. And then he moved on not wanting to be caught dawdling. He was finishing his drying off as Wick came into the room.

"Thomas, leave 'em clothes thar. We'll warsh 'em later. Head to yer room and look 'round. Might find somethin' ye need jest now."

Still wrapped in the drying cloth he hurried to the room. And there it was. A brown paper package with something written on it.

It read,

to: Thomas

frum: Yer frend

Thomas tied the cloth under his arm and untied the string from around the paper. He would save that paper, forever. Neatly folded and stacked one thing upon the other were clothes. Underwear was on top, then came a blue shirt, no two blue shirts, just alike. But one was bigger than the other. They both had four buttons to close them up and to keep out the cold. But the most wonderful thing of all was … they each had one marvelous pocket on the chest. Thomas could not believe his eyes! Wick was hollering about breakfast and he was ready to eat. Thomas's heart was pounding in his chest and his stomach was all a-flutter with amazement. On went the underwear, then the smaller of the beautiful blue shirts, and he could not believe what came next— a pair of denim overalls! He could not keep silent but began to dance around the room completely ignoring the blue patches on the knees of the overalls. This was too much! With his hands he rubbed his arms, which were now covered with this beautiful blue cloth.

He rubbed his thighs, unable to grasp that the whole of his leg was completely covered—all the way to his ankles and touching the floor. He could not help himself or hold back any longer! He flung himself across the bed declaring,

"Thank ye, God! Thank ye, God. Thank ye. Amen!" But he could not stand up just then as he was overwhelmed. Wick stepped into the room and as gently as he could asked,

"Thomas, 'ere ye alright?"

"Yes sir," came the sniffled response. The quiet sniffling continued until Wick spoke.

"I'm awful lonesome at breakfast this mornin'. How 'bout us men sittin' at the table. In the kitchen. I'd love ta have ye." He waited for Thomas to lift his head and look at him. "Bitsy an' me want ye ta stay. Always. But you kin decide fer yerse'f … who knows, my gravy 'n biscuits might kill us both … ye never know."

Thomas pushed himself up off of the bed, stood to his feet, and walked over to Wick. The boy never looked the man in the face but stood at the man's side and waited. Wick did not know what to do with the boy's silence. When Thomas let out a sigh of relief, Wick got his cue. The little eight-year-old boy and the husky man left the brown paper and the rest of its contents on the bed, and walked towards the kitchen. Then they sat across the table from one another and bowed their heads to give thanks. Each was separately thinking that he was the most grateful that morning.

29
Women

All day long, Wick and Thomas were together. Even while Thomas rested in the rocker on the porch, Wick was close by. But neither of them had much to say. As Wick showed Thomas the vegetable garden and pointed out the rows of beans and cabbage, Thomas either nodded his approval or grunted his disapproval. Wick was not used to these forms of communication, and he recognized that a grown man must not let his frustrations get out of hand. There was much to discover about this boy, and even more discovery was inevitable.

Bitsy was not around to confer with about these matters. He was on his own, and feeling quite uncomfortable. So he took the only approach he could think of. Ask questions. Who knows, he might get an answer.

"Thomas, have you ever been to a mill before?"

"Nope."

"My maw and paw lived here afore me and their maw and paw was here afore that. That's a long time, h'ain't it?"

"Yep."

Nobody could have known Wick's frustration. He propped himself up against the railing of the stockyard. Thomas stood looking down at his own feet in the freshly turned soil. Then it came to him.

"Do you have any questions fer me?" He was silently begging for a "yes".

"Well, I don't know what that word "birthin'" means. Is Bitsy mad at you or me?" He was still looking down at the dirt. Wick was lost for just a bit.

"No, she h'ain't mad at nobody. She's a midwife. When a woman needs he'p when a baby's 'bout ta be born, Bitsy's the one they call fer. And for Rosie. But the people's so spread out that they both have ta travel fur, fur away. Sometimes they don't git thar in time. The men git stuck with the birthin'.'"

Thomas was nodding again.

The boy seemed bothered by something, but he was not willing to talk. Maybe it was not a good idea, this question game. Wick moved on to the barn and gave a tour. The boy was still quiet.

Wick's solution was ... FOOD.

"Time fer beans and pone. How 'bout supper a little early?"

Wick did not intend to wait for a verbal response, and decidedly aimed his feet for the house. He paused only to fetch a fresh pail of water to carry it to the kitchen.

Thomas was following behind him, recalling what the doctor had told him about food. It still seemed wrong to eat food that he had not worked for. And to eat more than what seemed fair caused him to mistrust Wick. *How could 'his be right? Why would 'his miller man 'llow me ta eat what I h'ain't worked fer or deserved cause I was fam'ly?* All this considering was stealing his appetite.

He journeyed on. Something else was bothering him. *Maybe he could ask Wick what was meant by the writin' on the brown paper wrappin'?* He was insecure about what Wick would think of him. He should probably tell him that he could read. A little. He wished he could go to school. No sense in making himself more miserable than he already was.

Food was a good distraction from thinking so much.

This time, when they sat across from one another, it was Wick that said the blessing out loud.

"We thank ye, O, Lord fer this food. And the clothes. And bless them that prepared everthang. Amen" That was enough said about that. Wick really wanted to eat in peace.

"Kin we talk 'bout these clothes I'm wearin'? Whar did they come from. The writin' jest said 'frum yer frend'. I h'ain't got nerry a frend, jest my brothers ... Well, you know 'bout that."

"Yea, you bettcha! I know somethin' 'bout that. But hit'll have to wait 'til I'm done with the chores. An' with my eatin'. Now, let's have that spoon headin' towards that mouth a yern."

The beans, cornbread, and buttermilk were all satisfying to both of them, and Wick made it a point to smile at the boy across the table—the boy who had not smiled one time since he laid eyes on him. The discovery of Thomas at Founder's Tree would forever be etched in Wick's mind. Who could forget that blue coverlet? Its color was so unusual that it made every color seem pale compared to it. And as he looked at Thomas to make sure he was eating, his eyes landed on the blue shirt he wore. It was that same amazing blue. But that couldn't be.

If the chore list had not been so long that day, Wick would have stopped and gotten an answer about that shirt. But instead, Wick allowed Thomas to wash the dishes while he went into the grinding room to dust, sweep, and wash the window. Oh, and to take down the curtain that Bitsy had hanging for the winter season. He would have to wash that also.

Thomas finished the dishes and retrieved his clothes from the hearth. One piece at a time, he carefully laid them across his arm and went in search of Wick. He wanted to help wash those clothes. He wandered into the grinding room, not really paying attention to the voice of Wick. He was lost in remembering his previous clothes. His eyes and head dropped to consider his feet. What happened to his moccasins? He had worked so hard making them and taking care of them. Tears were trickling down his cheeks and in response to those tears, Wick put down his broom. He moved towards the boy hoping to be informed of the source of his tears. It was a waiting game.

"Thomas, did ye need ta tell me somethin'? I'm list'n." He was, sincerely.

"I made me some moccasins. But I cain't 'member whar they 'ere. Maybe I lost 'em in the mountains." He stood there, still looking down at his feet, then asked, "Who was it fount me?"

It was not time for chores.

"Hit was Bitsy. On her way to 'birthin'.'"

It was time for a walk. Wick had hoped Bitsy was going to be home when this time came.

He gently removed the clothes from Thomas's arm, laid them on the back of the kitchen chair, and picked him up to carry him outside. Wick carried Thomas up the road and began to point the direction Bitsy had taken that fateful day. Wick would only be able to tell him about the parts after she sent him to find him. He walked back to the house and placed Thomas in his bed. Wick's concern was not telling Thomas more than he could emotionally manage. Bitsy had warned him of going further than Thomas could bear. She was wise in these matters, and Wick wanted to protect this boy. Wick occupied Bitsy's chair while still relating the details of Thomas's rescue.

Thomas had been introduced to Timmy and Myrtle during the tour of the barn. These horses were part of Wick's storytelling. Even though Thomas's head was resting on his pillow, he kept his eyes open and watched the man's face as he told of the flying wagon on the road to find help. It was plain and clear. Because of the pain written on Wick's face, the journey down that mountain nearly wrecked the man.

But help showed up, Wick's face softened, and his voice gentled and slowed. Not much was retold of his night in the graveyard nor of Thomas's night with Rosie and Doc in the chapel. Lots of caution was used at this part of the story, for it was spoken in short sentences—and with a plain face.

But Wick could not leave out Brother Bill Downs and his wife, Mable. And he could not leave out the fact that an entire mountain had prayed, and had kept praying for the nameless boy fighting for his life.

At this point, Thomas had something to say.

"Was it them that gave me them clothes? The ones I wanted to warsh?" He had figured out that much of the story for himself.

"Yes, and they also sent lots a food fer ye. Doc was real werried 'bout how thin you was. I bet them women folk ere still askin' him if'n you've et up all they sent ye. Bless 'em. They wanted you ta live, and live strong."

They were both silent for a time.

"I'm glad she fount me. I'm glad ye got me well. When I was on that mountain, when I was runnin' fer my life ... I t'weren't sure livin' was a good idee. Seemed the whole Earth was a fightin' agin me."

It occurred to Wick as he looked on the face of that eight-year-old that all of them—Doc, Rosie, Bitsy, Brother Bill, that whole mountain full of folks—had been deceived. Thomas was most likely eight years old in body, but his spirit was much older. Too much pain—the physical kind, the emotional kind, and the mental kind—had been recklessly wielded at this child. And it was to be to the shame and ruin of one too many adults—the ones who had forgotten that Thomas's young life was precious, important, and to be protected.

"I think that's plenty 'nough rememberin' fer today. You have a good rest while I feed the stock and make ready fer the day ta end. If'n you want, I got a letter what needs readin'. After dinner suit ye?" Wick rose to make his exit.

He was almost to the door when Thomas called,

"Wick … that's yer name right?"

"Yes."

"Do you love her?"

"Yes, sir. All the time. Ever' day. Night an' day."

"I thought so."

And then Thomas's voice went silent, but not his mind. How long had it been since he had talked about his thoughts to a real person? He kept his eyes closed waiting for a memory of LOVE. *Mama said she loved me, but I never heer'd my father say that to NO one EVER!* Countless times, Thomas remembered telling his father he loved him, but all he ever received was a grunt or a "Git!" It was easier to say it inside his head, and then that stopped when Mama got sick. He only loved his brothers and sister. And Mama. *Oh, Mama, oh Mama, what happened to all the love?* A frightened boy lay choking on pointless questions. He shivered and pulled the quilt all the way over his head and kept swallowing.

Looking at Thomas over his shoulder gave Wick an instant insight. With the sight of those covers over the head of that tender, confused boy, Wick was then convinced that Thomas had not seen true, honest LOVE in a long time—maybe ever.

"How Ya've blessed me LORD over an' over," Wick whispered.

And how he missed his darling Bitsy this night!

30

Night Owls, Three

The stars were out, the frogs were croaking, and the crickets would not be silent. Those critters insisted on being heard. And in the kitchen, Wick could be heard. Thomas realized that he was very hungry, and he went straight away to see what kind of food or critter could be making such a racket.

And the smell! It hit him, slapped him in the face, and made his mouth water. Apples, bacon, and Heaven-knew-what-else was being cooked for dinner! But as Thomas got closer to the kitchen, he was met with the strangest of sights. Wick was wearing an apron, which was covered in brown spots. His hair was fuzzy and speckled with white dust. And his pants' legs were rolled up to just below his knees. Thomas could not hold back the laughter.

"Do ye need he'p? I could fetch Doc Williams fer ye." He was snickering at the sights in front of him.

"I'll thank ye ta mind yer own business. I spilt the flour, an' then I tried ta sweep it up. While the bacon was cookin' too fast and hot. Then I put my head in the oven ta check on the baked apples and burnt my hair just to please myse'f. After I put the fire out, I saw my boots was trackin' the flour dust all over creation so I went outside an' took 'em off. Furgitten that I furgot ta move that bacon outta the fire. An' so I grabbed that skillet bar handed and dropped the whole dad-blame skillet full a hot grease and burnt bacon in the floor."

Thomas was completely undone and laughter was spilling out all over him, Wick, and the messy kitchen!

"So's I cleaned what I could. Rolled up my britches' legs and was moppin' up the grease, jest 'bout got that done when I smelt them apples. But I got 'em in time. You jest caught me lookin' fer the good bacon I saved from the floor ... sit down." Thomas was holding his side that was delightfully in pain from this laughter.

Wick had dimples! And they were showing for all to see. No way could they be hidden on such an occasion as this! Life was in action, raw and silly and full of mischief. And delight.

"Proverbs is right! A merry heart doeth good like a medicine. We've both had a mountainous heapin' tonight, huh?" He was trying his best to talk through all their fits of laughter.

Thomas was still holding his side and trying without much success to catch his breath. Wick was in about the same shape. It was good to laugh even if it was at the expense of the bacon, the flour, and his own manly pride. It was precious to see that little boy laughing as if he had not a care in the world.

Despite the fiasco, there was plenty of good bacon, and the apples had not one black speck on them. The biscuits, which had been the leftovers of breakfast, had been toasted with butter. The two of them ate their food, talked very little, but worked hard at cleaning up. Thomas wanted to hear what was in the letter.

But Wick would have to bathe first, and Thomas was asked to wash the plates and cups and utensils. He mustn't lift heavy things. Doc and Wick had stressed to him the danger in straining his weak body.

Wick bathed quickly and reminded Thomas to take the lantern to the privy. So Thomas dried the last spoon, and placed it in its tray for the next day's use. And, with the kitchen lantern in hand, he started out the door to the outhouse. Wick was offering to go with him.

"We men have to stick together. I might need ye here ta make sure I don't break my neck or Bitsy's favorite butter dish. Heaven knows how dangerous hit is in this kitchen. Don't be long, now ... there's a letter waitin' ..."

A wonderful and bright full moon cast its beams of light on the worn path to the outhouse. But Thomas's mind was all a-jumble. Too much new information swirled around as he tried to get his bearings on what it all meant to him. Thomas had more questions.

What do I do now?

Whar are my brothers and sister?

What do these people want from me?

Whar'll I go ifn thangs go badly?

The hoot owl hooted his question to Thomas.

"Who, who!"

Who am I? He didn't have an answer. *Who were the Millers? Who really got me off that mountain? Who saved my life? And why?*

He latched his overalls. He picked up the lantern. He put one foot in front of the other as the owl continued its questions. "Who? Who?" Again who-who was its call. *Who's child am I? Whar in blue blazes do I belong?* Wick and Bitsy were taking care of him.

Don't know when I had so much food ta eat. And so many eyes watchin' ta see if'n I'd clean my plate. And them women fussin' and messin' with my stitches and my keevers. Like I was a baby! I h'ain't never seed a doctor a fore. But Doc Williams has truthful eyes.

He was back at the kitchen door where Wick was waiting. With papers in his hand. "Got this letter hur from Nellie. Bring the lantern to the hearth. Let's git yer warshin over with so's we can find out 'bout them new clothes."

Thomas scrubbed his face, hands, and feet. He dried them and then dressed for bed. Wick took up his post on the chair that Bitsy usually occupied. She was missed. Wick thought she might be back by dinnertime the next day, but he didn't promise.

The reading began.

Greetings,

I hope yuns 'ere havin' beautiful spring weather. I have had to take a surprising trip since I was with yuns. So much of what I'm going to tell ye is not about Thomas. I know he's doin' jest fine, though.

I want first to relate an important thing. When Brother Bill and I were making our way to my cabin after getting things settled at the mill, along the way, I found a blue coverlet in a mud hole. It was Brother Bill who told me where it came from. He remembered seeing it at the chapel the one time that Doc Williams let him look at the boy after the surgery. It was underneath Thomas's head. He remembered it plainly. He remarked that he had never seen anything as pretty as that blue cloth. And so, I was the one who wharshed it, and knew it might be better used to clothe the boy. I hope I have not ruined a precious keepsake. I did what I thought would be best.

I will continue with my surprises as they's several to relate. One day after I began to sew the shirts, I received a visit from Brother and Sister Downs. News was that there was a bad fever out Happy Holler way, and Doc Williams was several days there, and did need us all to come. I moved the goat to pasture, and as we set out, I left word with the Hoskins to gather the eggs and milk Buttercup.

None of us had ever been to that part of the Cumberland Gap before, but knew it would take days to get there. So we used the pony cart for most of the trip, but we had to leave it at the foot of the hill at a farm. They was only a little girl to tend to things as the fever had her Maw and Paw in bed. Polly was her name. She gave us a note from Doc telling us where to go next. Sister Downs stayed to tend to Polly's folks, and off Brother Downs and I went following the map.

It was near dark when we left the trail and we'uns had to follow with lantern the strings tied on branches left for us by Doc. We had to cross water three times and I almost fell in. Brother Downs had to stop and rest as the climb was steep. We passed a couple Indian huts but not a man, woman, ner dog was seed.

Doc met us with his light, and we walked across a little footbridge to a small cabin with its winders lit up. Hit was thar that we was told sad, sad, sad news. This cabin had seen death. We were the only ones who could hep bury the dead.

Brother Downs was to speak over the three graves, as the preacher could not be fount no whars.

Now, Thomas. I knowed you are brave. And I want ye to know that this tellin' is painful to hear, but the truth often is painful. Keep listenin' cause it matters to you.

The door of this little cabin came open and thar stood a little boy a lookin' at me and Brother Downs. He was crying. I knew I was needed. But I didn't know how bad it was.

There had been fever in the hills for three weeks, and so many of the ones that had died were of the same families. This cabin was a sad cabin fer sure. The little boy had lost his Paw, his Maw, and his only brother. And now he was alone with no relation to keer fer him.

Ned is eight, just had his birthday the week before we got there, but his Maw and Paw and older brother were took with chills and aches, and the such so bad that it was he himself who had to fetch the doctor.

And then Doc came, and then nothing could be done.

We spent the next day digging the graves. Ned was brave. He sang his Maw's favorite song. I nearly choked to death holding back my tears ... his voice sang so sweet. The song was Irish, taught to him by his Maw and Paw. Then I went to the cabin and tried to straighten up the mess in the kitchen and make a sensible dinner. But none of us had the mind to eat.

It was told to Doc by Ned's Irish parents as they lay dying that they was no relation what could take in the boy. Doc made a promise to find the boy a home with love in it, and he had to swear an oath that his promise to them was solid. They made him write out his promise and sign his name to it. They made a will and testament, and Doc was the one to make what was written in it happen. Brother Bill and Doc talked a long time about it while Ned and I packed his belongings.

We were sent away. Ned and I were sent back down the mountain, around the Indian burial grounds, and when we took a rest, we noticed that his cabin had been set on fire. Had to be done. Ned cried real hard then. He had to be growed up about it. We got to the farm all right and found the pony cart ready. Sister Downs is the smartest woman I know! And so we headed to over home.

Ned and I waited fer two days on them men! And lo and behold, what a sight they was. Both them men was covered in poison ivy, had it so bad they's eyes were swole up. I don't know who had it the worst … took both us women, Sister and me, and Ned to keep them men from scratchin'.

Well, Doc was truly sick. And it t'weren't from jest the poison ivy. Not enough rest and too much heartache was keeping him from getting well. Ned all but tied hisse'f to that bed and didn't let Doc go a wantin'g fer nothin'. He was a wonder and a help to beat the band.

As I was tellin ya 'bout the Doc. The next surprise goes like this. Ned was asked to read from Doc's Bible, the book of Proverbs, the third chapter. His eyes were still too swollen and blistered. Ned found the Bible and opened it, but he had to have help finding the proper page.

Well, some handwritten notes fell out of Doc's Bible. They seemed like they was thoughts writ down. Not wanting to be nosey, I picked them up and stuck them back in their place. Well, one had drifted under the bed, which I found later that evening just a'fore dinner time.

I told Joe, I mean Doc, about it and asked where he wanted me to put it. He asked me to read it to him. I just sat right down and comminced to readin'. All the words on that paper were about me—Nellie! They said he loved me. There it was right on that paper. Well, ya could'a knocked me over with a feather and then Doc said, plain as day, "Will you marry me, sweet Nellie? Will you?" And surprise, I said YES!"

We 'ere to be married this Saturday. Bring Bitsy and Thomas. Ned will live with Doc and me. God is good, and we are gonna make a fine family. But there is something to tell Thomas.

Thomas, Ned wanted you to know about the overalls. They were his brothers. We talked those first days about Thomas and the blue coverlet and how it got to my house. Ned was struck silent about the way Thomas was spared. He listened to me tell the story and of my plans to put that coverlet to its best purpose. He waited a long while to tell me his special want. Ned wanted you, Thomas, to have his brother Michael's overalls.

Ned had it in his mind that you could not go around in just your new shirt and under drawers!

But you will find the last of all the surprises in the blue bag, which is in with the clothing. Ned has written a note and hopes you like them.

Well, that's enough news for now. Tell Bitsy to bring the wedding cake! Hope all is well with you men. Doc will be out on a call, but hopes to see you all at our wedding.

Love and blessings to all,
Nellie and Ned and Joe

A blue drawstring bag was found and its note stated the marbles were Ned's. They were to play with, but to then bring them back next Saturday.

Good news at bedtime.

31

Generous

On the night before they were to go to Mournin' Dove Chapel for Nellie and Doc's wedding, Thomas helped Bitsy in the kitchen. He didn't mind that it was woman's work. It helped to keep his mind off the meeting of strangers. He was not keen on that.

Oh, he wanted to meet Ned. He wanted a face to go with his note on the brown paper and to say thank you in person for the other clothes. He had been working on a gift for Ned. Thomas had asked Wick for a knife to whittle wood with. He had lost his on the mountain. Somewhere. And so it was that Wick and Thomas whittled in the evenings after dinner dishes were washed.

Thomas was getting stronger, and he knew it. Bitsy said no matter what, she was not going to be break her word to Doc about having enough food for Thomas. And so, there was lots of tasty cornbread, baked apples, and fried eggs, at any time of the day. Thomas and Bitsy were in the kitchen waiting for the wedding cake to come out of the oven. He had finished washing the last bowl and been warned to walk softly out of the kitchen so as to keep the cake from falling. Thomas had never seen a cake before. Bitsy said this was to be a stack cake and that he could help put it together when it cooled. He was waiting …

Wick and Thomas got their baths and headed to bed at the same time. But Bitsy was going to be up late bathing and finishing the last touches on the gift she was making for the couple. Lace-edged pillow cases. She had been saving feathers for new pillows, and now there was a grand occasion on which to give them. Her best friend was marrying tomorrow!

The next morning, Timmy was hitched, the wagon was loaded, and Thomas and Wick were seated, waiting for Bitsy. Seated in its own wood box between the adults was the enormous stack cake—treated like a baby. Thomas had his own wood box to sit on … and this time, this journey made without Mama, was made for a happy reason.

As if Thomas could be happy. He desperately wanted to go home. He wanted with all his heart to be going for a wagon ride headed to his own home. The wagon moved down the mountain road. It was headed in a direction that Thomas knew was not going to take him home. There was no such place. Something told him that he was so far from the home cabin that it would be impossible to ever return. Impossible.

And still, he was remembering his first wagon ride. He closed his eyes so that he could see those faces again. Ralph, Ross … Oh, where were they? How could he get to them anyway?

It was Bitsy calling his name. She was telling him the names of all the people who were likely to be in attendance. He wanted so much not to be going where there were strangers. He didn't like them. Didn't trust them. Most strangers were dangerous.

Bitsy left him to enjoy the rest of the trip in peace. She was talking to Wick about the new settlers moving in to the holler. And then they were at the chapel.

"Thomas, most likely folks will know yer name without you havin' to tell 'em. Today's 'bout our friends gettin' hitched, so I don't think you'll be bothered much. Look, I think Ned's on the church house steps lookin' fer ya."

It was true. Ned was looking right at Thomas and making his way through all the adults to get to him.

They stood looking at each other. Thomas reached into his pocket for the gift.

"Ned, thank ye fer the clothes and the note. Hur's yer marbles … I made ye sump'in … it's in the bag with yer marbles."

"Yer welcome … I cain't write too well, but I'm learnin' … Can you write? I'd like ta git letters from ya … Cuz I don't know no other boy …"

Thomas had been thinking on how it would feel if he himself had no brothers or sisters. It felt like that was the truth, anyway. Ned would be really and truly alone. It was a good thing that God was giving Ned two people to look after him. It was a good thing.

It was time to go inside the chapel. Ned, with his wide shoulders and chubby frame and brown shaggy hair, walked behind Thomas. Thomas with his small thin shoulders, slight frame, and golden brown curls, walked behind Bitsy. And she behind Wick. And they all walked through the chapel doors, proceeded down the center aisle, and filed into the very first row.

Thomas did not tell anyone, not even Ned, but he had never been to a real church house before. Just a schoolhouse. And only a few times. But he knew instinctually to be silent. The ceremony began. There was a preacher, and Brother Bill was standing beside Doc Williams. And there was Sister Mable standing beside Nellie. Doc looked Nellie in the eyes and repeated what the preacher said. Then, Nellie took a turn. Doc then put a ring on Nellie's finger, and the preacher said, "I now pronounce you man and wife."

And he kissed her right in front of everybody!

During the celebration, Ned and Thomas took the marbles and played almost silently by themselves. Most of the people at this wedding were old or were tending to crying babies. When it was time to cut the cake, the boys names were called and they reluctantly came from behind the chapel to oblige.

Eating the molasses stack cake was fun! Answering questions was not. Both the boys had numerous mountain folk asking them if they knew so-and-so down such-and-such gap. It was tiring, for the answer was always NO. Then it came time for Thomas to go back to the mill. Ned was going to stay with the Downs for a few days while Nellie and Doc Williams were setting up house. Ned asked Thomas if he knew what setting up house meant. He didn't know, either.

Bitsy and Nellie hugged and cried and hugged and cried. Wick and Doc Williams shook hands and patted each other's back. Then Nellie and Doc road away in a pretty buggy pulled by a shiny black horse and wedding gifts overflowing the back seat of the covered buggy.

The scene reminded Thomas of the day they buried Mama. All the buggies parked under the oak trees—but none of those buggies were as pretty as Nellie and Doc's.

Wick helped Bitsy onto their wagon seat. Then came a helping hand for Thomas to be seated on his box. Ned was standing with the Downs on the chapel steps looking at Thomas, and waving good-bye with the blue drawstring bag on his wrist. Thomas would never forget this day. Or Ned. Or the chapel.

32

Trust

The couple could not wrap their minds around the questions they were living through with Thomas. Wick certainly knew what Bitsy was thinking without her having to say a word to him. He felt the same way. The same pestering feeling invading his confidence seemed to be written on her face. *Does he know what it's like when someone ya love won't trust ya? Ta know that no matter how kind or thoughtful or he'pful ye ere, why, they cain't believe thar's enough goodness to make 'em believe?* What was the next right move, for Bitsy and Wick were feeling defeated and saddened with each passing day. Bitsy's log of information got folded and put in her pocket. Wick's head hung low and still. His and Bitsy's eyes did not meet often, but their work-worn hands often found each other and gave firm squeezes in unity of heart and purpose.

Thomas went through the motions. Undressing, night dressing, washing, waiting. He was not hungry. He was not sleepy. He was not angry. He was not … He dropped down on the bed, then put his back on the straw mattress starring at the ceiling, at nothing. He felt nothing. His thoughts were mechanical and uncertain. *Tommorry I'll get up, warsh, eat, and do garden work. And then the next day, I'll do the same. And the next, and the next. And then they'll be so tired of my eatin' their food and doing' nothin' to earn my keep that I'll git th'owed out … or given away to the next fam'ly that feels sorry fer me. I jest about can lift heavy stuff, so I must be gettin' well. Then what? Maybe I best get a plan ta leave a'fore …* Thomas stopped in mid thought. Someone was coming. A gentle tap, tap, tap sounded on his door.

"Thomas, can we come in?" It was Wick asking.

"Hit's yer house, don't ask me," he mumbled back.

Although these two adults had no children of their own, they were not able to disconnect from obvious need, and they could not stand for neglect of any sort. They wanted to make Thomas feel loved and safe. But how, in God's precious name, could they make their heart's desire any more clear to this boy?

"Shall we play a game a'fore we get our rest?" Wick winked at Bitsy in an obvious way. "I'll go first." Bitsy took her seat, and he paced the floor at the foot of the low trundle bed. "My most favorite memory ... let me think ... oh, how 'bout that time you and me was fishin', Bitsy, and I caught that feisty ole catfish, was pullin' him in, and plumb forgot my boots was still on and went right in that water with 'em on! You remember how you laughed at me so hard that ye fell in yerself? Huh, you 'member?" Bitsy was all in at that recollection.

"Well, if'n hit's my turn, that ain't my favorite. Mine's the time Nellie and me was pickin' blackberries down behind the chapel." She looked Thomas right in the eyes. "We musta been 'bout ten or 'llebum. Well, we was not 'pose to leave the house but she got ta talkin' bout dunplins, and how she wished she had some blackberries and next thang I knowed it, we was out tha door and on a search." Oh, how she wished Thomas would show some sign of enjoying this new game. "Well, we found 'em and picked em' and e't way too many, but what the problem was, we furgot 'bout not leavin' the house and the why of it. Ye see, Nellie's Maw put two loaves a bread in the oven we was a'pose ta take out while she was cannin' at the neighbors down tha road. We ran that long trail back to the house, but hit were too late. Black smoke was already comin' out da winders, and we knew then we was in trouble." She waited for him to ask questions. But he was silent. "Can ye guess what we had fer dinner?" Silence. "Well, we had blackberry dumplin's a'course!"

Both adults waited for some response. "What's yer favorite mem'ry, Thomas?" Wick had started this game and was pulling up his stool to listen. But there was a blank look on the boy's face. But they waited anyway.

"I ain't got no fav'rites. I don't like 'his game. I cain't win cause I ain't able to play."

It was not what they had prayed for. *Oh, God he'p us he'p him,* Wick desperately and silently prayed.

"Would it he'p if'n I asked ye questions 'bout yer brothers, 'ere ye sister?"

The silent pleading with God continued.

"I don't wanna remember, I cain't."

"That's alright. No harm in tryin'. 'Ere ye too tired to talk? We want ta git ta know ye." Thomas shrugged his little shoulders. Bitsy took a swing. "I can remember some a their names. Brooks, Baby Toy. Um, Margaret is yer sister, right?"

He nodded then took a breath, "Ross and Ralph."

"Which one is the oldest?" Wick was asking this one.

"Ralph."

"And is Margaret next?"

"No, Ross is … then Margaret and then me."

"Then Brooks and Baby Toy!" Bitsy felt triumphant.

"I got a mem'ry, but it ain't funny or my fav'rite. When they lowered Mama into that hole, Brooks took his stick and hit them men." Wick patted Thomas's leg.

"They's hard thangs that happens to us, Thomas. Thangs we don't want ta happen, ever. To no one especially the ones we love. I'm sorry fer the sad thangs that have come yer way. I cain't save ye from that pain, but if'n you'll let me and Bitsy, we can love ye and he'p ye until yer growed 'ere yer fam'ly comes lookin' fer ye."

"And we'll always love ye even if that happens." Bitsy was doing her best to keep things moving in a peaceful direction.

"Can I ask questions? I ain't got the words all sorted out but I got ta know. If ye get a baby, 'ere ye gonna give me away?" Wick wanted to shout his answer but caught the words before they escaped. Bitsy silently but sweetly shook her head, no.

And finally Wick spoke. "What would ye do if someone ye loved never trusted ye or believed ye loved 'em even thought ye told 'em a hun'ered times and showed 'em ever nice way ye could think of that ye was always gonna love 'em?" In earnest, Wick waited for a Thomas answer. He was willing to wait all night. But that would not be necessary for Thomas spilled out his answer and put some emotion behind it.

"I wouldn't stop lovin' … EVEN IF THEY DIED—I'D STILL LOVE 'EM!" That was all he needed to say. It made him feel safe to have said it aloud. And then Wick stood and paced at the foot of the boy's bed slowly, turning to look at Thomas's face.

"That's what Bitsy and I've been tryin' ta tell ye, Thomas. We want ye ta stay. We want ye, jest like ye are. And it's okay if'n ye don't love us, we can understand. But they's got ta be an undertandin'. We just want ta love ye, and keer fer ye, even when ye git so big ye could take keer of yerse'f."

He waited for the boy to respond. Bitsy was gently holding Thomas's left hand. Wick moved himself and his stool to hold his other hand. It was quiet for some time. And then Thomas spoke, "I don't want ta go away. I been askin' God what ta do next. He ain't answered yet. So fer now can I stay? Yer saying I can stay, right?" And there was LAUGHTER all around that bed.

Thomas was staying. For now.

33

All This and More

WHISPERS. *Voices so quiet one can't be sure that words have been spoken. But could you possibly know the struggle within when you have made a decision that turns into a mistake—something that can never be undone? And you must live with the knowledge, the whispering voices saying, "LIFE cannot ever be the same … LIFE cannot ever be the same" … between them and you … until Eternity.*

Down at the post office on John Barnett Mountain was a list. There were several lists, to be precise, but one in particular was famous. The famous list was the EXPECTING LIST. If a woman was expecting a baby, you could put your name on the list, along with the suspected day of reckoning, and Bitsy Miller would make a call. Oh, the expectant one had to leave her directions using landmarks or personal markings so she could be found. And if that expectant mother couldn't read or write—why, the Post Master would know all about her! And then the whole mountain would be informed.

Back at the Miller's homestead, the garden was robust and well-looked-after, the mill was grinding, and Bitsy was canning and drying berries and the like to enjoy in the winter. Thomas was chasing the rooster and using his slingshot to knock the thieving blackbirds right off their roosts. No corn for them! He was learning quickly to spot raccoons, too. He also had permission to eat cucumbers or tomatoes any time he wished. He was still a mighty too slender!

It was on such a day that a note was found in the crack of the mill's door. It had Bitsy's name on it, and so Thomas, having found it, brought it to her. She was frying green tomatoes for breakfast.

"Who could be sendin' me a note?" Her eyebrows squeezed closer together. Then she moved the skillet off the burner, and grabbed

Thomas by the shoulders. "We've got to go. And go now!" She was shaking him with every word.

Wick had already loaded the wagon the night before and left at first light to go to the general store in another town farther down the Gap.

Bitsy continued, "I'll have to rely on you, Thomas to be my he'p. I'll go pack my birthin' bag and you git yer extry clean shirt and put it in a sack. I'll need all the he'p I can git."

That was too much to take in all at once. Thomas had to run everything back through his mind as he walked to his room. "Ya never know what'll be happ'nin' from minute ta minute," he replied. He found his extra shirt and was looking for a sack when Bitsy hollered to get Myrtle ready. Although Thomas had watched Wick countless times hitch Timmy to the wagon he, Thomas never participated. He didn't know the order of business, and the best he could do was lead Myrtle out of the barn. And that is exactly what he did. With his extra shirt rolled up and tucked under his arm, he made a beeline for the barn.

And he stood there just a blink before recognizing what was going on. A baby was coming! "Myrtle and I are going to help with a birthin'. But why me?" Bitsy was at his back and delivering orders.

"Now I got this end. You go make us a food bag with enough for the day while I get my little cart hitched. I'll meet ya at tha gate." Off he ran, leaving his shirt with her, and maneuvering his legs and feet to go as fast as possible. An apple, a chunk of bread, a little ham, and two boiled eggs. But what about a water jug? Under the washtub. With everything tied up in an old tablecloth, he snatched up the jug and headed for the well. Bitsy was just driving the cart toward the gate.

"Open the gate, shet it after and jump in!" Just like that they were on an adventure.

Thomas was 10 years old now, but the Millers often forgot that. No school teacher had come to those parts, so Thomas spent most— no, all of his time—at the Miller's. But they were good to him, and he was glad to be safe. Rarely did those old memories of abuse and neglect come visiting. Of course not until … Thomas was in the woods, away from the Miller's house, in unfamiliar surroundings. Wick and Bitsy had been careful and protective of Thomas. He always had one of them near him at all times. But just now, he had to get hold of himself.

Bitsy's words just then provided some comfort. "We are going to a rough neck of the woods, Thomas. I never heardt of this woman in my life, but Rosie sent word that they was gonna be twins and tweren't no man or woman to he'p with the birthin'.

She'll be all alone and hit's probably gonna go siderways. We have to go past Founder's Pass and past the Indian settlements, but they's nuttin' ta be a'feared of, I promise." She knew Thomas's reluctance to meet strangers.

A real adventure. It was years ago when last he encountered an Indian. This adventure was starting in the daylight, yet he was not going to be alone like the last time he was near an Indian.

Myrtle plodded along, and Bitsy and Thomas whistled and sang together. Even when the road got rough or altogether undetectable, they kept on singing. It was a great day for traveling. Not too hot, not too cold, not too scary. It was not even scary when they had to get out of the cart to move logs or look for the best trail to use. Yes, it was fine—until it was not. Bitsy was biting her lower lip. Thomas was gripping the side of the cart and trying not to look how close the wheels were to the edge of the drop off when a young girl appeared ahead of them on the mountain road. He was shocked at what he saw and Bitsy was breathing a sigh of relief.

"Yer almost there, ma'm. The lady Rosie told me ta tell ye ta git along as fast as ye dare! I'll ride with ya and guide ya." Thomas could hear her telling Bitsy to look for the smoke rising on the hill ahead.

Myrtle was encouraged to pick up the pace, and they all jogged and jiggled up and over those hills until they stopped. The girl hopped out, said goodbye, and scampered out of sight before Thomas could squeeze out a goodbye to you! The cart jogged on until a whoa and a thump! They had arrived. Thomas had had to ride backwards facing the entire trip as there was not room on the short driver's seat. His head had banged hard at the abrupt stop. But hard was not the right word for what they were about to face.

A woman's voice was calling for help. The voice was calling in such a way as to testify that it did not believe that help was ever going to come. But the voice did not give up.

"I'm here Darlin', I'm here! Bitsy's my name, and this here's my boy, Thomas. He's a dear, kind soul and will do us both a world of good ..."

"That's who I am! I'm Thomas Alva Good!" It was an under-the-breath discovery, but it had sound! The sound of belonging! "She just called me "her boy," and said I was a dear kind soul and that I'm good. I'm GOOD!"

"THOMAS, THOMAS! COME FAST!"

He ran into that shack, left its door wide open, and witnessed a sight he could never have dreamt. Bitsy was throwing blankets and metal things out of her bag and blood was puddled under the woman—the stranger.

Bitsy was using her sweet, convincing voice. The one she used when something was really important for someone to understand. The one she used when he, himself, was confused or discouraged. She was pointing to things and aiming her words at Thomas. He was able to hear and take action. Clean water, lantern, pillow, string. Success. Next she needed more light and more water. The woman in pain told him where to draw the fresh water. He ran to that well and tried not to slosh too much of it on his way back.

Bitsy had rolled up her sleeves and her skirts and had Thomas tie them out of her way and then she washed—no, she scrubbed—her hands. Tops, bottoms, in between the fingers. And while she was scrubbing, she was telling him to do the same.

Next, Bitsy had lain down on her stomach and pulled at Thomas's hand to join her. "Thomas, this here's Rebekah, Becky for short. And you and I are going to see about these babies who are puttin' up a fuss about who's comin' ta see their Mama first." She was handing Thomas a lit lantern.

He didn't know how heavy lanterns could get when they're having to be held for forever! Becky's face was colorless, and Bitsy's face was completely consumed with focus. Her hands worked wonders while he could hear her praying under her breath. But awesome was the next sight.

First there was a sobbing followed by a panting and then a tiny, tiny hand. Then tiny shoulders and a tiny pink face. "Thomas, set the lantern aside." She handed a tiny wrapped form to his ready hands. "Tell him yer name and keep him warm." He was so lost in the experience that he didn't notice that the woman was silent and that there was another baby announcing its arrival. Thomas was instructed to pull up a chair and was handed the other wrapped infant. Bitsy was so busy, but he was her boy, and he was doing good for them all.

34

A Good Name

The sun was rising, and the shack was struggling so hard to brighten. Most of Bitsy's form was in shadow. But her spirits were high, and the feeling in the room was bright and warm and inspiring. She hummed and whistled and bustled about the one-room shack that Becky called home, doing her best to make things different. It was natural to want to make it different from the harsh reality of abject poverty and honest, obvious abandonment.

They had made it through the night, and Thomas Alva Good had worked in tandem with Bitsy to stay the hand of DEATH. The twins, a boy and a girl, were certainly tiny—but alive. Yet, they had no names, and that made Thomas uneasy. He tried not to notice that the mother had not moved in hours, but he was uneasy.

Thomas interrupted the whistling. "Will Doc Williams have to come?"

Bitsy came closer to him to answer. "I think Rosie has already sent for him, and maybe, just maybe, he'll be here this morning. I pray it's this morning. Right now would be wonderful." But there was no sign or sound from him. Only the new babies were making a sound, however weak it was. Thomas thought it was wonderful.

He had slept off and on in that straight chair holding a baby in each arm. There was nowhere to sit, and only one cupboard and one table in the entire space. It made him wonder if the woman had even wanted the babies, for there was not one sign of preparation. Maybe there was a box somewhere hidden that had all the things the babies would need. He wondered. And listened to make sure the twins were still alive. It was altogether worrisome.

Bitsy would spell him when she could. There really wasn't anything to talk about, and Thomas hated to break the beautiful sound the twins were making. Ever so gently, their breaths broke the silence. But Thomas remembered that babies are not usually quiet for long. Something new to worry about. What were they going to do next? There was breakfast to come, and lunch, but not much hope of food. Bitsy was a wonder in the kitchen, but he had his doubts—this time.

The next time he saw Bitsy she had in her hands a box—a box lined with a blue cloth. A cloth that looked remarkably like the same cloth as his shirt. It was his shirt and it lay on top of the old tablecloth from the mill. "What's that fer?" He hadn't caught on.

"It's the babies' bed, silly. Lay 'em in one at the time." She lifted out the shirt first. "Now we can keever 'em up and find ourselves some vittles."

The box was placed on the foot of the bed without disturbing Becky. And as Thomas and Bitsy were looking at the babies, the door cracked open. What a welcome sight! Both Doc Williams and Rosie slipped in, each carrying a wooden crate.

After the hugs and hellos were exchanged in whispers, Doc went to work with Rosie right behind. Thomas was excused from the proceedings and sent outside to wash up and ready himself for breakfast out-of-doors. This gave him plenty of time to scout around. Doc's wagon was tied close to theirs, and Thomas instinctually went to get the animal's feedbags and to draw water for them. Taking care of the livestock was a special privilege, Wick said. It wasn't long until his food was brought to him. He was ready to eat, and Bitsy was ready to talk.

It was apparent to her that Becky's man had left a long time back and maybe didn't know she was expecting. But that wasn't the main trouble. Becky was in need of help—help of every kind. Because the delivery had been rough, Becky was too weak to speak. Doc and Rosie were going to take care of her for now. They were free to head home anytime what pleased them. Thomas told Bitsy that he wanted the babies to have names. But they were not in charge, as she reminded him.

So after some conversation with Doc and Rosie, and some signing of papers, Myrtle carried them out of that hollow and back toward the mill. They were almost home when Thomas made a sharp whistle, stood up, turned to face forward and spoke in Bitsy's ear.

"Bitsy, I heered ye tell Becky that I was yer boy. And it made me proud and happy, but what it mostly did was made me remember. I 'membered my whole name. Thomas Alva Good, spelt G-O-O-D. I even 'membered that. My Mama's name was Sarah Jane Good. I still don't know my father's name. But he's as good as dead to me anyhows. Seein' he hain't looked fer me neither here ner thar." For the first time since coming to the Miller's, he rested his head on Bitsy's shoulder with both his arms around her neck.

35

Nearly Grown

And so a couple more springs and winters passed at the mill. Wick and Bitsy never got to have a baby of their own. And yet they never took for granted the preciousness of life, nor did they ever presume upon its length. Never did they waste an opportunity to be examples of honest love, and never did they quarrel about petty things. With two exceptions—Bitsy's flowers and Wick's orchard.

Wick needed to prune at the right time, and it seemed to always come at the time when her roses and dahlias needed fertilizing. And poor Thomas was caught in the smack middle. He had grown wiser than expected, and his silence was often mistaken for indifference. The truth was that he was thinking—studying, as he called it.

Thomas loved books, and though they were scarce, the Miller's did their best to get what they could, borrowed, loaned, or traded. Most of the reading was difficult for him. He hated to ask for help, but sometimes there was nothing else to do but to acquiesce. He didn't know why it bothered him so, as the Millers were always willing to help. Wick even said helping Thomas made him smarter, and that was a compliment. But as Thomas matured, he realized his need for change and for finding his own way in the world. There was nothing wrong with being a Miller, if that was interesting to him. Why, he and Wick had long talks while Wick smoked his pipe and Thomas mindlessly whittled on insignificant chunks of wood. But Thomas still could not picture himself as a Miller. He wasn't a kid anymore. He was nearly fully grown now. He felt that he was as strong as any man—except Wick. Still, it was an enormous comfort to think of Wick as that father figure—invincible, protective, and loving to a fault. But Thomas knew Wick wasn't always wise—especially where those trees were concerned.

Bitsy was as steady a woman as ever. She never tired of birthing babies and growing things in her gardens. She still winked at Wick's silly antics and pretended to be angry when her men stole away to fish. She did not wink at the changes that were occurring in her relationship with Thomas. Though the changes were a must, she felt that pain of not being needed in the same way as before. It was obvious that Thomas was a young adult now, not a needy, injured, and starved eight-year-old boy. While these necessary changes were often in the air, they weren't welcomed. Like most mothers, she was not friends with that change—often she prayed about this enemy.

Although every season must bring its shift, many of Bitsy's preferences remained the same. She continued to purchase new fabric every spring for a new dress. And she still insisted that all her flowers be in bloom when she wanted them. She also insisted that her Christmas trees weren't complete without a bird's nest in them. These consistencies year after year helped ease the pain of change—but the comfort above all comforts was that they all three loved each other through everything.

Most of Thomas's thoughts these days went from question to answer to new question to new answer. A few questions that did not have answers remained. For example, when Wick put an advertisement in some mountain newsletters asking Thomas's family's whereabouts, there were no answers. Years had gone by. Wick had even paid to have his siblings' names put in print to see what or who would turn up and not one response. The Miller's address had been listed. No letter ever came. Thomas's past had been erased.

Since that day without Mama, his whole world had been turned inside out. What was once his was no one's, and what he did not want for a time was all he received. Bad on good. Evil for good. Sour for sweet. Pain for tenderness. For a TIME, it seemed that Cauldron's stench was always in his nostrils. Haunting him and taunting him to give up. But TIME can change a thing. It can shape a man's thinking and his purpose. It can, if LOVE lives in his soul. TIME can make sense of jumbled, jagged pieces of life if HOPE is allowed to smooth and sand and

reshape a man's heart. And if real PEACE is invited and encouraged, a man can rise up to be more than those hideous, stealing, lying ingredients the Evil Accuser delights in using. But it comes at a price so high that if one had to pay it all at once, it would kill a man. It would snuff the life right out of him, and all would be lost.

But Thomas was never really lost. He was not forgotten, and season after season, first flower then fruit began to bear witness. He was small of stature, but not of character. And just like an orchard willingly going through its stages, Thomas was budding and hidden fruit was erupting.

It was on a ritualistic trip to the post office with Wick that Thomas heard of the opportunity. He checked the handbill to verify the details.

> New Settlement needs Farmhands
> Weekly Pay
> Good Hours
> Merry Moore Mountain Developers
> Contact: Ben Cooper

Was this a good idea? Ta go ta work in someone else's fields fer pay? What would that get me? How fur was Merry Moore Mountain? Thomas would write a letter requesting information and answers to his questions. That was all he could do. And when the letter came, he would read it, consider what it said, and talk it over with Wick and Bitsy. Oh, that will be a heavy consideration. But he must try something. Something must change!

It should be acknowledged that no young man likes to wait even for a known reason. Waiting is mostly painful, and yet LIFE makes all men take their turn waiting. Knowing that one must wait for something unforeseen, something not imagined or described can make a heart sick. But that is the way of man.

If life had taught Thomas Alva Good anything, it had taught him that GOOD things do come. The wait can be drawn out, but there is HOPE!

Because two people said yes to the sick boy wrapped in stormy threads of NEGLECT and ABUSE, a LIFE was saved. That boy would in return LOVE and HONOR their unselfish gift. He loved them as best he could, but knew LIFE would have its seasons of change. Wick and Bitsy became instruments of HOPE and PROMISE for the TIME Thomas would indeed need to believe in himself. The game of LIFE was afoot, and he was no longer afraid to step out and see what his future days without Mama would become. Yes, he was without Sarah Jane Good, but he was not ALONE. His God had seen to that!

Epilogue

The life adventures of Thomas Alva Good included a wife, children, a home built with his own two hands, apple orchards, both vegetable and flower gardens—and love aplenty. He was a pure Appalacian Kentucky Pioneer. He is my maternal grandfather. I, as his granddaughter, think that perhaps he wanted his family to know that neither mother nor father can produce any security of value. If we could have talked, he might have told me that siblings may stand to protect, or at best help at times, but all humans fail us. I know he would have said that death makes its appointment with everyone.

He would have also wanted us to grasp that daily success is often tied to the work of our hands, but worth and meaning are not. Struggles in his life served to prove that God's loving and personal hand was upon the very thoughts and breath of Thomas.

As I examine Thomas's life, I see that what seemed impossible only brought forth beauty because Thomas chose to believe God instead of the ugliness that often stared down at him. Thomas had strength of a unique time. The strength drawn from a deep source, like a well to be used to give life and rest. Thomas could see life and death deeds each day played out. Yet, his same strength allowed him to laugh at himself and his inadequacies. It also allowed him to know the hope in knowing the living God who took such care to create Thomas Alva Good—for reasons we will know only in eternity.

I can still recall the last time I saw Grandpaw Good. I was four years old, and he was dying. I didn't know he was dying, but as I entered the darkened bedroom where he rested, he asked me a question. He wanted to know if I wanted to trade a piece of butterscotch candy from the dish on his dresser for a silver dollar. I was happy to make that trade. He put a smile on my face as he said, "Thanks little girlie."

Thomas Alva Good resides in Heaven. I still have my 1921 Liberty silver dollar. I still adore butterscotch. My time on this Earth so far has had its challenges, but I am not alone. I too know the generous, loving God. The same Father who rescued Thomas has rescued me.

No, I was not there that day, that day without Mama, but Thomas was. All the days without Mama served as a type of FERTILIZER for the soil of his LIFE, so that the STRENGTH of his seed would have great impact on this world. Those seeds were "watered" with the LOVE that flowed from his God, his real Father.

About the Author

Beth is the granddaughter of Appalachian Kentucky coalminers.

Her Kentucky heritage is rich in folklore and saturated with haunting stories of hardships and triumphs.

She moved with her family to the suburbs of Atlanta in the mid-1970s. Beth spent long weeks every summer and most school holidays visiting Happy Hollow and Cannon Creek back in Kentucky.

She married Jim Dukes, and together, they raised six children, along with the occasional extra two or three that snuck in at dinnertime. Beth used her gift of storytelling and her love of old black and white movies to enrich her children's education and their sense of adventure.

Her love of fabric and old books keeps her young. Or maybe it is the three grandchildren—or is it four or five? Jim and Beth currently reside in Spring Hill, Tennessee.

Notes

1. Poor Wayfaring Stranger, author unknown, FolkSongIndex.com, www.stephengriffith.com/folksongindex/poor-wayfaring-stranger, (accessed March 1, 2018).

2. Amazing Grace, author John Newton, 1779, Public Domain, www.easysonglicensing.com, (accessed March 1, 2018).

3. My Jesus, I Love Thee, words by: William Ralph Featherstone, 1864, music by: Adoniram Judson Gordon, 1876, Public Domain, http://www.simusic.com/worship/hymns, (accessed April 5, 2018).

Acknowledgements

The journey of publishing this book would not have been possible without the following people.

Thank you so much to my editor, Loral Pepoon, and self-publishing guru, Kayla Fioravanti of Selah Press. Kayla, keep writing those books and blogs and wearing those different hats! Loral, I have gratefully benefited from your Heavenly gifts.

There aren't sufficient words to express my emotions when viewing the artwork involved in this adventure. God bless you Moriah, Christine, and Stephen.

I'm so grateful for my Aunt Lori, Aunt Marty, Uncle Ross and all the Good people.

I would not be who I am today without my dad and mom, Vernon and Mary Miracle, who knew when to leave those hollows and who knew how to give life a chance outside of those sad hills.

I could not have embarked on the writing of this book without Generous Jim Dukes, my husband and gift from God.

I thank God each day for my wonderful children, who teach me every day how precious life is and bless me unspeakably.

I give warm gratitude to Lona Fraser and Heartprint Writers Group for all the many words of encouragement and for making me comfortable enough to read Thomas Good's story out loud.

BJ and Dorie, Cindy, and Jerry, thank you for all the ways you told me and showed me I could do all things through Christ.

And most of all, I offer my humble gratefulness to the Lover of my soul, my God and my Savior, who woke me from sleep to tell me the story of little Thomas Alva Good, my grandfather.